To Glenn & Roberta

JD thinks you will
appreciate these stories

Mary Morley Kalergis

# CONSIDERING ADOPTION

BOOKS
by Mary Motley Kalergis

*Love In Black & White*
Dafina Books

*Charlottesville Portrait*
Howell Press

*Seen and Heard: Teenagers Talk About Their Lives*
Stewart Tabori, & Chang

*With This Ring: A Portrait of Marriage*
The Chrysler Museum of Art

*Home of the Brave*
E.P. Dutton

*Mother: A Collective Portrait*
E.P. Dutton

*Giving Birth*
Harper & Row

# CONSIDERING ADOPTION

PHOTOGRAPHS AND INTERVIEWS BY

## MARY MOTLEY KALERGIS

ATELERIX PRESS
288 Park Avenue South
New York, NY 10003

Photographs and text copyright © 2014

ATELERIX and design are trademarks of Atelerix Press,
the publisher of this work.

For information about special purchases, please contact
Atelerix Press Special Sales at contact@atelerix.com

Text font is Bembo.

FIRST EDITION

Designer: Kemper Conwell

ISBN-13: 978-0-9899263-5-5 (Atelerix)
10 9 8 7 6 5 4 3 2 1

*As it was in the beginning,*
*is now and ever shall be—*

To David

## ACKNOWLEDGEMENTS

I'll be forever grateful to the families in these pages, who were my guides
along the way as I set out to document the experiences of adoption.
Their courage to share their truth was matched only by a generous enthusiasm
to introduce me to others who had so much to offer this book.
I also want to thank my husband David and my son Hugh,
who encouraged me to enter the new world of print-on-demand publishing.
Without their support and guidance, years of work might still be
sitting on my desk gathering dust. I also am grateful to my designer,
Kemper Conwell, who had the ability to make real my vision
of this book as a family album.
—Mary Motley Kalergis

# INTRODUCTION

••••••••••••••••••

*CONSIDERING ADOPTION* is a combined road map/travel guide to the emotional landscape of adoption. Unlike other books on the subject, it won't tell you *how* to adopt. As important as this subject is, it's well covered in existing books and on the internet, with expert guidance available from professional counselors. This "how" changes regularly, as new laws are passed throughout the fifty states, and foreign countries open or restrict access to their available children. As complex as these topics may be, accurate and timely information is accessible to those who do their homework.

Less available, because it's less tangible, is comprehensive information about what it really feels like to adopt a child. This is understandable because there is no way anyone can tell you what it will be like when your day comes. You'll get that phone call or letter telling you the moment has arrived and that a child is waiting for you somewhere. And you'll enter, or perhaps re-enter, the world of parenthood in a way unique to you and your family. No one can tell you what you will feel or what you will experience emotionally. But that doesn't mean there's nothing you can do to get ready.

A wise traveler doesn't begin a journey without preparation, most especially finding and studying a map. If those who went before have left a record or guide to their journey, and you have that record available, your trip can be better, safer. This is true even, or maybe especially, where the journey is emotional rather than physical. For that kind of journey, each of us needs all the help we can get.

For a number of years I lived as a documentarian in the world of adoption, toting my cameras and tape recorder around the country, meeting and talking with people of all ages and from all walks of life. I sought them out, or they found me, because they had lived through some important aspect of adoption. When I asked if they would share their experience with others in pictures and words, their willingness to reveal themselves and delve into their most intimate feelings was inspiring. Each person in these pages speaks for them self, but can also be seen to represent a point on the eternal triad of adoption: children, parents who adopt them, and birth parents who have relinquished them. Some people may play more than one of these parts. And a few chosen souls have, no doubt, played all three parts in one lifetime.

That triad provides the background for our map of the emotional landscape of adoption. Think of it as the *terra firma* of the continent being explored. The triad shows itself in many forms and is experienced in many different ways. No one can tell you how *you* will experience it. But others who have been there can share *their* personal experience, in all its trembling anticipation, heartbreak, joy, disappointment, and exquisite fulfillment. Through their generosity and willingness to be photographed as well as interviewed, we are given a rare opportunity—to gaze into their faces while they talk to us about something important.

As we look and listen, a number of themes emerge: motivations for adoption, the search for identity as a parent or a child, the act of relinquishment, single parent adoption, special needs adoption, open and closed adoptions, and more. This book takes its structure from these themes. If you, the reader, want to get the "lay of the land," you can spend some time looking at the Table of Contents, noting the themes which make up the *Parts* of this book, and how they relate. Or you can just dive in. No magic is claimed in the placement of individual stories within the greater structure. Most of these stories could fit comfortably within other *Parts* of the book. But, as in life, choices must be made, and this book is organized in a way in which, I hope, justice is done to the power of the subject and its themes.

**Part One: Infinitely Varied and Beautiful** opens with a look at the ways in which individual adoption stories unfold. First, David and Nancy describe their struggle with infertility and the almost mystical circumstances that led to the adoption of their daughter, Talia. Next, Richard and Jill discuss watching the mysteries of nature and nurture unfold as their adopted daughter, Sophie, exhibits traits and talents hitherto unknown in their family lines. Charlie and Jude share how opening their hearts to their adopted children has helped heal their own childhood hurts.

In **Part Two: Into the Firestorm**, two families describe the events and resulting sensations of being thrown headlong into the most tumultuous episodes of their lives. No adventure story or work of fiction can match the drama as life-changing events unfold for these everyday people. From these stories, we also get an introduction into other themes that will continue throughout the journey—in particular, the agony of relinquishment and the potential for psychological damage to children who have been in too many foster homes or experienced prolonged institutionalization. These shared stories allow us to be forewarned. No matter whether they are a birth parent, an adoptive parent, or have been adopted themselves, few in the triad ever seem to escape completely unscathed from the act of relinquishment and its aftermath. And romanticizing the act of adoption can leave the adoptive parent perilously unprepared for possible difficulties that may be encountered when a child from a disturbed background enters their home.

With that cautionary note, the stunning paradox of these adoption stories must also be acknowledged. While the possible damage from relinquishment and institutionalization is recognized, many of the stories here present an opposite occurrence. Relinquishment sometimes leads to immense gratitude on the part of the adopted child, and a child adopted into an American family from a foster home overseas may well make the transition totally happy and well-adjusted from the moment they enter their new life. One of the most important lessons here is that since we don't get to choose the results from our choices we need to have the courage to face all the possibilities.

In **Part Three: Motivations**, families share their reasons for adopting. Infertility is often, but not always, the initial motivator. For some, infertility is not the issue. In every case, however, the motivation can be traced to the fundamental power of an elemental life force—the desire to be a parent. This power is awe-inspiring in its strength and, sometimes, its apparent irrationality, even when it's not being considered in the context of adoption. When the force of this power remains unrequited, perhaps for years, the power of its drive is unimaginable to those for whom it has been easily satisfied. Knowing this is key to understanding the risks and the hardships that adoptive parents are willing to undertake.

Adoption practices have changed tremendously over the past decades and the shame and secrecy which once surrounded it have largely been banished as useless relics of the past. **Part Four: Open and Closed Adoptions** introduces the topic, which re-emerges in other interviews throughout the book. Suffice it to say that the trend towards more open adoptions appears to be a healthy one, as truth triumphs over secrecy in healing the human heart.

It takes two people to conceive a baby, but only one person to be a parent. **Part Five: Single Parenting** reflects this reality, offering both cautions, encouragements and role models for those who would pursue this path. As with other themes throughout this book, single parenting is

integral to many of the adoption stories told in other *Parts*, but the subject is important enough to be worthy of its own segment.

Likewise, **Parts Six** through **Nine** explore the topics of multicultural and mixed race adoptions, adopting many children, children with special needs, and adoption in the LGBT community, even as many of the themes discussed therein could just as easily have placed them elsewhere.

**Part Ten: Foster Homes, Orphanages and Institutionalization** deals directly with the possibility that an adopted child may arrive with psychological damage attributable to neglect or even abuse from their past. Some of these stories may be difficult to read, especially for those families in the process of adopting. Will they experience the same difficulties? Do they dare risk it? Can they stand up to it? The power of the life force and the desire to parent often overcomes the reluctance of taking on the "too difficult" or the merely impractical. And some people, as will be seen, actually embrace the hard cases. Even where there is not a special calling, the parenting of children with psychological damage seems to carry the potential for rewards as vast as the magnitude of the difficulties taken on, whether intentionally or inadvertently. As with the physical act of childbirth, the beginnings can be painful, but the pain usually recedes with the passage of time. And the parent may well then be ready to do it again.

**Part Eleven: Relinquishment, Abandonment and Self Esteem** continues the exploration of places tangled and dark—especially for those who have relinquished a child or have themselves been relinquished. For while we will encounter birth parents and adopted children for whom relinquishment is "no big deal," for countless others it is an overriding constant in their lives, never far from the forefront of consciousness. Every adoptive parent needs to realize and appreciate the magnitude of the decision or circumstance which made their adopted child available to them. This is not because of some theoretical doctrine of implied fairness. Rather, there is a good chance that relinquishment issues will arise in their own "intentional family," no matter how many barriers are erected to deny or keep these issues at bay. Again, forewarned is forearmed.

**Parts Twelve and Thirteen, Roots and the Search for Identity, and When Biological Families Reunite**, continue the exploration of adoption from the point of view of the adopted child and the birth parent. This is not to slight the role of the adoptive parent—far from it. These stories may, in fact, be particularly helpful to adoptive parents who wonder if they've done enough, or worry that their child's interest in their biological parents is abnormal or a reflection on their parenting. As these stories point out, nothing could be more natural than for an adopted child and a birth parent to be curious about each other. In some cases they may be more than curious, they may be obsessed. This can be understood as a counterpart to the adoptive parent's innate drive to parent. When frustrated, this drive to know more about one's birth child or birth parent can increase to an intensity reaching the unhealthy. For an adoptive parent, understanding their adopted child's interest in learning about, and perhaps meeting, their biological family can bring positive relief. Just as having more than one child doesn't dilute the love within a family, it is clear from these stories that adopted children have room in their hearts to encompass the entire triad which makes up the boundaries of their existence.

Ultimately, all the stories told within these pages demonstrate that nothing is more healing to the human heart than truth tempered with compassion. The tragic fact is that some hurts may never heal, but, in far more cases, the triad of adoption—the parents who adopt, the children who are adopted, and the birth parents who have relinquished them —can form a unity bordering on the spiritual, fulfilling the needs of everyone involved and leaving an abundance of love for others.

*—MMK*

# TABLE OF CONTENTS

• • • • • • • • • • • • • • • •

**Part Three: MOTIVATIONS**

**Part Four: OPEN AND CLOSED ADOPTIONS**

**Part Five: SINGLE PARENTING**

**Part Ten: FOSTER HOMES, ORPHANAGES AND INSTITUTIONALIZATION**

**Part Eleven: RELINQUISHMENT, ABANDONMENT AND SELF ESTEEM**

# PART ONE:

## INFINITELY VARIED
## AND
## BEAUTIFUL

# DAVID AND NANCY WITH TALIA

•••••••••••••••••

**Nancy**: Once we decided to get married, I immediately started thinking of starting a family. It never occurred to me that we wouldn't be able to get pregnant. But after ten years it was obvious that we'd have to consider other alternatives for becoming parents.

**David**: We tried different fertility treatments, but ran out of money and enthusiasm for that road.

**Nancy**: We both came to feel that a biological child wasn't meant to be. We felt like the Lord had a different plan for us. Once I decided on adoption, I was completely OK with the prospect.

**David**: I felt the same as Nancy, except I did strongly believe we should adopt a child from America instead of overseas. There are so many kids here that need loving homes, I didn't think we needed to travel half way around the world. I particularly liked the idea of adopting a local child who needed a family…

**Nancy**: …and one day he handed me a newspaper and said, "Read this."

**David**: There was an article about a newborn baby– she'd been found outdoors right here in our area, alone and abandoned by her birth parents. The unusual circumstances of Talia's birth were even on a national television show, but no relatives ever came forward.

**Nancy**: In that same newspaper article, there was information about how to become a foster parent and adopt through social services. We went through the training to prepare for foster care, which you have to do in order to adopt through the county agency. A lot of the program is a test to see how committed you are to being responsible for a child.

**David**: It was the best thing we ever did. It's tough and demanding and we learned a lot about ourselves.

**Nancy**: You have to write a biography, and they have you write a letter to the prospective child and birth parents. To get your foster care license, your house has to be up to code and you have to be trained in CPR. With background checks, including fingerprinting, the whole process took six months. Once we graduated from the program, our name was put in the county's data base, which made us eligible in the entire state. Of course, this means you're directly competing with that many more prospective parents when a child is available to be adopted. The hardest part was the calls before we actually got to bring our daughter into our home. It was heartbreaking to know we were on the short list and then not make the final cut.

**David**:  The social workers see a lot of horrible stuff. Their first priority is to place each child in the best home possible for that individual. Still, it was painful every time we'd get close to parenthood but not get there.

**Nancy**:  From August until December we were tossed up and down with excitement and disappointment. Then, on December eleventh, Dave got a call about Talia. He called me at work and said, "Don't even ask any questions. This is our child." Her foster parents had her for five months because there were no known birth parents to relinquish her. The foster mom knew that it was in the best interest of the child to get her in a permanent home and was finally able to convince the authorities. The miracle is that we were the ones chosen to adopt her, this same baby we'd read about months ago, who started the whole adoption process for us. Of course, we had no idea that she'd look like me. We chose the name Talia for her, because it means "dew from heaven." We also named her after my mother and kept the name the emergency social worker gave her when she was found abandoned as a newborn. We had to get her a court-ordered birth certificate from the state using her approximate age when she was discovered.

**David**:  I go back and forth about her birth mother. I sympathize for what she must have gone through, but at the same time she did just toss her aside with no seeming regard for her survival.

**Nancy**:  I blame the guy involved. I sometimes wonder if he didn't tell the birth mother that he was going to place the infant in a safe place, then panicked and deserted her.

**David**:  We'll never know, but I do sometimes think about it.

**Nancy**:  We had to wait another six months to legally adopt her. That was a happy day. There were at least fifty other families in front of the judge. It was like the happiest party you can imagine, for all of us.

**David**:  The social workers, the judge, everyone, were as happy as the new parents. After all the heartbreaking things they have to deal with, "adoption day" is when they see the good they do.

**Nancy**:  I was forty seven years old by the time we finally got to adopt Talia. Being older parents, we sometimes get tired, but we're also mature enough to be more grateful than perhaps a young person could ever be.

**David**:  We went through years of fertility treatments, trying to have a child. And then, there in the paper, was a story about an infant with no family or home. At that moment I knew we were meant to adopt. What I didn't

know was that months later that same baby would be our daughter, Talia. She's a gift from God.

**Nancy**: God often takes a long time to let His will be known but He does come through. Raising Talia makes our life so much more meaningful. I no longer question why I'm here or what I should be doing. Being Talia's mother answers all of that. The fact that she survived on her own those first days after she was born confirms that she's destined to have a special purpose in life. Our purpose is to give her a safe and loving home, so we need her as much as she needs us.

# RICHARD AND JILL WITH SOPHIE

•••••••••••••••

**Jill**: When Richard and I decided to get married twenty years ago, I knew it was unlikely that I'd get pregnant. I'd been married previously and gone through a lot of fertility treatments with no resulting pregnancy. My first husband wouldn't consider adoption, even though I was all for it….

**Richard**: …whereas, from the beginning of our discussions about family, I was perfectly willing to adopt a child. In fact, it was an appealing idea.

**Jill**: So we put our names on the waiting list at an adoption agency as soon as we were committed to getting married. Richard's openness to adoption helped convince me that he was the right guy for me! When we got the call that our baby was waiting for us, we were so excited and happy, so thrilled to finally hold her in our arms. It's hard to imagine more joy. It was a sudden immersion into parenthood that changed our lives forever.

**Richard**: I was never hung up on keeping my genetic legacy through the generations. In fact, after we got Sophie, and it became apparent how beautiful and smart she is, I'd joke that she obviously comes from better stock than us! Her birth mother was playing three varsity sports and her biological father was a gymnast. By the time Sophie was a year old, it was clear how athletic she was. She'd catapult all over the place, doing flips and high jumps from the time she could walk.

**Jill**: Sometimes I jokingly say that maybe we've improved our line through adopting her.

**Richard**: My great-grandfather and grandfather were both rabbis. One reason I was inclined to adopt a girl was because I didn't want our son to have pressure from my family to follow a more religious path. Shortly after we got Sophie, however, we did put her through a Mikveh.

**Jill**: It was such a mysterious and beautiful ceremony, with three chanting rabbis and Richard and Sophie in a pool. As the mother, I only observed.

**Richard**: It mattered so much to my own mother, I realized we couldn't deny her that comfort.

**Jill**: Both Richard and I are more interested in the arts and progressive politics than we are in Judaism. But still, we honor our parents. When Sophie was small, both our mothers were a great help. Adoption is so much easier now, when there's no stigma, no reason for secretiveness. We videotaped every step of her coming into our lives including being in the judge's chambers when she was several months old.

**Richard**: That doesn't mean that being adopted doesn't come with its own set of issues. When Sophie would get mad at us, she'd say, "My other family is rich and has brothers and sisters for me! They would let me do this," with "this" being whatever it was we had forbidden her to do.

**Sophie**: I grew up knowing I was adopted, so it never seemed like a big deal or made me feel different. My parents are my parents, just like anyone else's. Sometimes people come up to me and say, "You look just like your mom"…

**Jill**: …which always astounds me.

**Richard**: An even stranger comment is, "She doesn't look like either of you." As if the possibility of adoption doesn't exist.

**Sophie**: I am curious about meeting my birth mother one day. When we talk about genetics in biology class, it makes me want to see what my birth parents look like. Not because I don't know who my real parents are,

because I do—they're sitting right here, the ones who raised me. My therapist thinks I want to ask my birth mother why she gave me up, but the reason seems pretty clear to me. I don't take it personally.

**Jill**: I think her analyst tends to-over examine the fact that she's adopted.

**Richard**: Well, that's what he's trained to do—look at family dynamics. He clearly thinks Sophie's issues have to do with feelings of abandonment by her birth parents.

**Sophie**: That's just his opinion. I don't feel abandoned at all. I'm sure I'm better off here than I would be with my birth mom, because she was single and young. My biological father doesn't even know I exist, so how could he have abandoned me? I feel lucky to have the parents I do. For you guys, I wasn't an accident.

**Richard**: When we adopted Sophie, we were so ready to have a child and we've never wavered in our love for her.

**Jill**: If we had a biological child, we might be more prone to expectations of the same strengths and weaknesses that we have. An adopted child is a blank slate. It's so interesting to watch Sophie develop.

**Richard**: And endlessly fascinating. Watching Sophie grow up has brought me into realms I never expected. The pride I feel watching her on the basketball court is something I probably never would have experienced if we'd been able to get pregnant. Whether its dance,

horseback riding, or gymnastics, her teachers all tell us what a natural she is. She also has an innate sense of style that she certainly didn't get from me! We suspect she's always looking at our clothing and hair style choices with a critical eye. Sometimes, she'll insist that I go back inside and change!

**Sophie**: But academics don't come naturally to me. That's one thing I wish I had inherited from somebody!

**Jill**: She has some learning disabilities that make school more challenging. She works hard at school, though, and does well. We're proud of her. Sophie's terrific not only in sports, but also in dance and the visual arts. Once she gets to a college which appreciates her strengths, she'll excel.

**Sophie**: But when it comes to academics, I can't concentrate. My mind likes to move around just like my body does.

# CHARLIE AND JUDE WITH CHARLIE, JR., BRANFORD, CLARENCE, RONALD, BRIJADA AND LARISSA

• • • • • • • • • • • • • • • •

**Jude**: Charlie had children from a previous marriage, so when we got married sixteen years ago, we started right out with kids. It was always understood we were going to have our own. We got involved with People Places which facilitates foster care and adoptions. Charlie grew up in foster care and I was adopted. We both wanted to be involved in therapeutic foster care, to help kids who, like ourselves when we were young, really needed a home. Charlie had three siblings growing up, and they were often separated in foster care. We wanted to take in kids with their siblings because we believe brothers and sisters should stay together. Our first placement was a lovely sibling group of three. After a year we were all so attached that we wanted to adopt them. But a family member of theirs wanted them, so we stepped aside. It was painful. We'd fallen in love with those three kids. We still keep in contact with them.

**Charlie, Jr**: I remember them, too. Blood couldn't make us any closer. But then I remember that summer after they left. I was in Florida with a friend when my parents called and said. "We have a surprise for you when you get back." I'm thinking maybe I'd get a new bicycle but when I got home there were three new kids at the front door waiting to greet me.

**Jude**: We wanted to make it a family decision, but sometimes children need a home sooner rather than later. We knew Charlie supported our vision of helping kids who weren't as fortunate.

**Charlie, Jr**: I've never had a problem sharing my parents with kids who need a family. I was about ten or eleven at the time and the kids were younger than me. I liked being a big brother and role model—I still do. Having people look up to me for guidance helps me be a better person,

**Jude**: The other children in the family often determine whether a placement is successful. If they aren't on board, it's not going to work.

11

> Opening my heart and my home to these kids has healed so many hurts in my own life. It's brought me to a wonderful place of fulfillment and gratitude. Loving these children and each other gives our lives meaning. —Jude

**Charlie, Jr**: Kids spend more time with each other than they do their parents. It's important that everyone is happy with the arrangement.

**Charlie**: We've been so blessed with Charlie. He's an exceptional young man. He's always been there for the younger kids.

**Jude**: Yes, as our oldest son, he sets the tone for all the children. We still do foster care, as well, so there are often new faces at the dinner table. My husband and I don't look at our foster care activities as something for just the two of us. It's a family affair. And since our three youngest were adopted through the foster care system, they know how important it is to help others in the same situation.

**Charlie**: Jude does an incredible job. She's a full time Mom, dedicating all her time to our children. Which, of course makes it easier for me when I come home from work, because the children are healthy and happy.

**Jude**: My husband isn't giving himself enough credit. He's a great dad. There's no way this family could get along as well without him. I can't overstate how much better it is for kids to have both a mom and a dad.

**Charlie**: I was in and out of foster care growing up because my mother suffered from bipolar disorder. She'd be hospitalized for months at a time. So it was hard for her to take care of all four of us. It was also hard to find a foster care home where we could all stay together.

**Jude**: I came to America when I was four years old. I have a vague memory of being in an orphanage before that. I was adopted by an American serviceman and his Korean wife. My adoptive parents divorced about a year after we were back in the States. My father had custody and never talked much about either my biological mother or my adoptive mother. She was deported back to Korea and I was raised by my adoptive father and his mom. I grew up in an African American home, one of the only Asian people in the entire county. I never saw anyone who looked like me until I was in third grade! I considered myself African American but didn't really think about it much. When I reached my teens, though, I felt like no group wanted to claim me. I went through different phases, all over the place, trying to figure out where I belonged. Many kids that age do, but, because of my particular situation, my experimentation was pretty pronounced.

**Charlie**: After we married and had a couple of great kids, we felt like we wanted to make life easier for kids who were less fortunate than our own. Both of us had rough childhoods and we felt blessed by our current good fortune. We wanted to give something back.

**Jude**: I teach parent skills at People Places and we take in kids who need immediate foster care. One of the great things about People Places is how careful they are in placing the kids in a family with the right dynamic. For example, our three youngest are very active so they

fit right in with our other kids, who are always involved in sports.

**Charlie**: I'm developing software for people who are interested in foster care and adoption. It will help them work through the system and offer advice for problems. The program can help parents understand their kids' behavior, whether they're adopted or not.

**Jude**: Kids don't come with an instruction manual, so parents need all the help they can get!

**Charlie**: Families who adopt through People Places get eight weeks of training before they take the kids home. And they're always available when problems arise.

**Jude:** Opening my heart and home to these kids has healed so many hurts in my own life. It's brought me to a wonderful place of fulfillment and gratitude. Loving these children and each other gives our lives meaning.

**Charlie**: The church is the other cornerstone of our lives. It's where we get our focus and direction, and gives us

hope and joy. I grew up on the streets of the projects. I wasn't exposed to Christian values and I got in trouble. There was one lady in the neighborhood who watched out for me. She was always there when my Mom was sick or I was sent from one foster home to another. There are angels out there, definitely, no matter where you are.

**Jude:** I had one of those angels in my life too. She took in foster kids and mentored me in both fostering and Christianity. People who get involved with others, who really put themselves out there, are the ones with the most contented hearts. Serving others and living in obedience to God's laws is the key to a worthwhile life. A common thread that runs through our family is that each of us is interpreting God's Word and walking in obedience. Our children know that they are truly loved and never alone. We tell them, "We're not doing you a favor. Loving you blesses our lives in a greater way than anything we give to you. It's not an effort. It's like a heartbeat."

PART TWO:

INTO THE
FIRESTORM

# CHRIS AND KIM WITH ANNIKA SIENA

●●●●●●●●●●●●●●●

**Kim**: After I'd tried to conceive for over a year, we went to fertility specialists and discovered that the problem was with me and that I wasn't a good candidate for IVF. Adoption was something familiar in my family. I had a foster sister and an uncle who were adopted. When I brought up the subject with Chris he agreed without hesitation. He said, "Sure, if that's what we need to do, let's do it!"

We contacted a lawyer specializing in adoptions. We liked her right away and she told us about a birth mother who hadn't placed her unborn child. She said we should write the birth mom a letter saying why we would be good parents. We went home and I poured my heart out in that letter. Then Chris worked on it, adding pictures. The next day we brought it back to the lawyer, but three days later, on my birthday, we got a call saying that we hadn't been selected. A few hours after that, we got another call. The other couple had a last minute problem and we'd been chosen to adopt this unborn baby after all.

We talked to the birth mom for over an hour by phone that night and she agreed to meet with us. She was living with her mom and her five year old daughter, hundreds of miles away. I found that Annika's birth mother was someone I could respect. She knew she wasn't in a position to take care of another child, so relinquishing her second child was a real sacrifice of love. She called once a week during the last six weeks of her pregnancy and as soon as she was in labor, she gave us a call. Soon we got another call telling us that our daughter had safely arrived. We hopped in the car at five that morning with our hearts pounding wildly. We made what should have been a nine hour drive in seven. There was no time to linger. We wanted to see our baby girl.

When we entered the hospital room, her birth mom was there holding her. We sat down and she put Annika in my arms. This beautiful newborn looked up at us with her angelic face and Chris and I were gone—we were both instantly crazy in love with her. Then it got really hard. The biological mother was having second thoughts.

> When we entered the hospital room, her birth mom was there holding her. We sat down and she put Annika in my arms. This beautiful newborn looked up at us with her angelic face and Chris and I were gone—we were both instantly crazy in love with her. Then it got really hard. The biological mother was having second thoughts. —Kim

Both her mom and her older daughter had been with her when Annika was born, so it was an intensely emotional time for their whole family. The birth mom left the room while we were holding the baby but, soon after, she returned with her own mother, who said, "I think it'd be best if you left now." Our hearts sank. We knew that she felt the same attachment we did and it was going to be beyond difficult for that family to relinquish the baby.

We went back to our hotel room in shock. Eventually we got a call that everything was on track, that the birth mother had just been having a hard time. We were so torn between our love for that little baby and our empathy for her birth mother.

**Chris**: It was probably made even harder for Annika's birth mom because she was breastfeeding. All those early nutrients are good for the baby but it made it extra hard for her to relinquish her baby.

**Kim**: We came the next morning to complete the paperwork for relinquishment. We were told that the adoption was still moving forward but the birth mother didn't want to see us. We felt so sad because we wanted to give her some gifts and bless her for what she'd done, both for us and our new daughter. After we'd filled out the legal forms, we learned that the birth mom wanted to be alone with her baby. They'd call us when we were supposed to come back. Again, we were terrified that

she'd change her mind. But a few hours later we got a call from her mom, who said, "We want you to know that we love you. Even though she's having a really, really hard time, in my daughter's heart she knows this is the right thing to do."

It kept getting harder. We got another call telling us not to come to the hospital because the birth mother still needed more time. Finally, someone from the hospital called and said we could come over. Annika's birth mother had put together a little album of her pregnancy and blood relatives. It was so sweet. The last page of the album was a picture of me and Annika at the hospital, with the inscription "Thank you, Kim, for being Annika's Mommy". Everyone was crying. I was flustered when the hospital made me sit in a wheel chair in order to release Annika from the hospital. But I sat and they placed her in my arms and wheeled us to the car.

She was only six pounds. Neither Chris nor I had a clue what to do. Most parents have nine months to prepare. We had six weeks! Because she was so small, the doctor told us to make sure she ate every two hours. We couldn't stop looking at our watches!

**Chris**: The next morning we met with a social worker for breakfast. The other patrons were amazed that we'd have such a tiny newborn at a restaurant. It was a long story to explain to strangers, so we just smiled.

**Kim**: Though it had only taken seven hours to get to the hospital, it took much, much longer to get home. We'd pull over and feed her a bottle every two hours! It took us every bit of fifteen hours to get home. And she was so little, her diapers were leaking everywhere.

**Chris**: We had to stop and buy preemie diapers. We didn't know whether to laugh or to cry. What an emotional roller coaster ride!

# DAVID AND CAROL WITH ALEX AND NATALIE

••••••••••••••••

**David:** We'd talked about adopting children since we first got married. We always knew that if we wanted to raise a family that would be how we'd do it.

**Carol:** It's not that there are any medical reasons we can't have children…

**David:** …at least that we know of.

**Carol:** But there are so many children who are thrown away. And Dave and I have so much love to offer. Why bring another child into this world, as evil as it is, when there are so many children who need homes?

**David:** We'd been married seven years before we even talked about having a family. Then, two years ago, we were vacationing in Puerto Rico…

**Carol:** … sitting in a hot tub, having a drink, when a conversation about having children just started spontaneously. It was such a romantic setting to talk about our future together. And here's an amazing thing—Natalie was born in Russia the very day that we made our decision in the hot tub. A friend had recently adopted from Russia and when we got home we talked with her about it. We started the process on January 2 and our two children were in our home by June 15.

**David:** Carol gets the credit. She handled all the paperwork. The day something would arrive in the mail she'd fill it out, have it notarized, and send it back immediately. By the time you get over there, you've seen photos of the kids that the orphanage has selected for you after reading your application. Thank God they didn't present us with a room full of children to choose from. That would be heart wrenching. Most people immediately feel a bond with the kids presented to them. We certainly did.

After meeting the children and agreeing to adopt them, you have to go back to the States and wait for several more months. Meanwhile, of course, you're filling out more paperwork. Then a court date is set up in Russia and you return for the formal adoption proceedings. The orphanage had guest quarters for us as adoptive parents and provided a driver and translators. We gave Alex and Natalie the middle names of our translators as an acknowledgement of their heritage.

**Carol:** Meeting our children for the first time was like no other experience I'd ever had. Never, ever. There was an immediate overwhelming bond. The hard part came later, when we had them on our own. The first night the kids slept over with us in Moscow, Natalie screamed so loud and long that the housekeeper came to the door. She bundled Natalie up really tight in a blanket and bounced her up and down, hard. That worked for her, but I never could get the hang of it.

The flight back to America was horrible—the worst thing in my whole life. Alex wouldn't let anyone buckle him into his seat. He must have been restrained in the orphanage and he wanted no part of it again. Even though he was supposed to be potty trained, he wet himself repeatedly. And he screamed non-stop on the entire fourteen and a half hour flight. Natalie was no happier.

When we finally got through customs at JFK and had transferred to La Guardia, we discovered that our night flight was cancelled. By now I was in tears, along with the two kids. Alex and Natalie threw such a fit at the hotel that someone called security. They didn't offer to bundle and shake the kids like they had in Russia! The flight home the next day wasn't any better. Thank God my parents were there to help us when we finally made it home.

I got in the shower and let the warm water wash over my tears, thinking "What have we gotten ourselves into? Have we've ruined our lives?"

It took months to make sense of things. I'd quit my job and no longer had my friends from work. I went from being able to come and go at will to being completely overwhelmed. I didn't feel like a mom. I felt more like a caregiver, and a not very competent one at that!

**David:** For me, feeling like I was a father grew gradually, over time. They called me Dad, but I felt like there were little strangers in our house. When I confided to my brother-in-law how I felt, he asked, "Have you changed a diaper?" When I said "Yes," he laughed. "You're a dad!" he told me.

**Carol:** In the beginning Alex didn't speak a word of English and was terrified of our dogs. I had to lock them in the garage. Our household was completely upended. I tried to find a parenting class, but nothing was offered unless you were pregnant. If you're adopting two children from a foreign orphanage there should be a required class on how to deal with the issues. I sure wasn't prepared for the conflicting feelings I experienced in the first six months of settling into motherhood. I felt panicked, cornered. Then I felt guilty about feeling that way. It was overwhelming.

Grocery shopping was a nightmare. The first sentence Alex learned was, "May I have it?" and he said it constantly. To this day, Natalie still screams if I want her to ride in the grocery cart. She needs to be carried everywhere. I have to remember that at seven months, when we first

got her home, she couldn't even sit up or roll over by herself. In the orphanage, the babies just lay in their cribs all the time. Alex still needs a lot of physical contact as well. It's as if they're making up for all the hugs and kisses they missed.

That first week, Alex locked David in the garden shed twice by shutting the door when he was in there. We finally removed the latch so it couldn't be locked from the outside. When he wasn't screaming in terror over the dogs, he was so careful and so quiet. He'd take down one toy at a time and carefully box it back up when he was done. When we first got them home, Alex would wolf down food like it was his last chance. Natalie would suck down her bottle like it was her last meal. Now they're more picky eaters, since they can take their time.

It was a real adjustment for Dave and me, settling into parenthood. I tried to make time for him, for us, but the first half year I didn't have much left after the kids' needs were met. He told my mother, "When I shut that front door in the morning to go to work, I'm on vacation!"

You can control things at work, but with young children, forget it! You can make all the plans you want, but things seldom work out the way you planned. Now the family has settled into a routine and life is a whole lot more manageable. Maybe you just get used to having to stay flexible! You let go of the fantasy of motherhood and become comfortable living in the reality.

PART THREE:

MOTIVATIONS

# DANIEL WITH HIS MOTHER, PALI

**Pali**: My husband had worked with Mother Theresa in India before we got married, so we had a connection with that orphanage. One day we went into DC to deliver medicine and clothes for shipment to the orphanage and we met a liaison who told us about some of the children there. Our biological son, Gabriel, was only seven months old at the time. We'd thought we wouldn't adopt until he was older and that we'd get a little girl. But the moment I saw Daniel's picture, I knew.

*That's my son*, I thought. *What is he doing in India?* There wasn't any decision to be made—by the time we got home that day, we knew that we'd adopt him and that we would call him Daniel.

**Daniel**:  The nuns at the orphanage were my mothers. Even though I didn't have a father, I was surrounded by love. The worst punishment they doled out was they'd lash you with a rose stem, with the thorns removed. Even that didn't happen often because the Sisters were very indulgent with us. We didn't have toys but we always had other kids to play with.

When I was six, the Sisters told me about an American family who wanted to adopt me, and they gave me a photo album filled with pictures of people I'd never seen before. I didn't even know what a family was, much less an American family! The more I looked at these pictures from America and heard their letters read to me—translated into Hindi, of course—the more attached I became to the idea of them raising me. I especially longed for a father.

I'd never seen newspapers or magazines, much less TV, so I couldn't even imagine my future, speaking another language in another part of the world. I had no idea that I was going 9,000 miles away or that I wouldn't be returning. The last time someone came to adopt me, they had brought me back. It didn't occur to me that I wouldn't be back again!

I was amazed by the taxi ride, but was just in awe in the airport and on the airplane. The thirty-two hour flight was beyond my comprehension. It was almost like being reborn, leaving that orphanage in India. It was my first time being in the big wide world. I wasn't afraid because the woman from the adoption agency and my best friend Maria were both traveling with me. Maria was being adopted by a family in Minnesota. When we got to JFK and they separated us, I got upset and started to cry. Maria was my best friend and my last link to India.

When I first saw my parents, I recognized them right away from the photos. But when the lady from the agency turned to leave, I freaked out. I hadn't known her for long but she was more familiar to me than the people from the photographs and I was a long way from anything else familiar. I yelled and screamed. Airport security stopped and questioned us, because it must have looked like a kidnapping!

**Pali:** I had made a scrapbook for him with pictures and stories so he'd be familiar with us when we picked him up at the airport. It was heartbreaking to hear him cry out for his escort. He was screaming so loudly, we were desperate to distract and comfort him. So I bought him a chocolate Santa Claus at the gift shop. As soon as he started eating the chocolate, he calmed right down.

**Daniel:** Hey, chocolate is the universal language! I remember the beautiful white flakes falling from the sky. Of course, living in India, I'd never seen snow before. I also remember them popping that piece of chocolate in my mouth and the instant relief it gave me. I thought, "Hmm, this family thing might be OK after all!"

**Pali:** Until he could speak English and tell us about it himself, we had no idea he'd been previously adopted in India and returned to the orphanage. They made him sleep under the house and treated him like a servant. It was like a horrible fairy tale. The mother wanted him, but the father and the three other sons didn't and he was treated like a dog.

**Daniel:** I still remember how it felt being returned, and also how hard it was when the Sisters in the orphanage transferred every two years. I longed for stability but it took a while to trust that my new American parents were a lifetime commitment. Even today, I sometimes have real commitment issues. It's hard to believe that people won't turn their backs on me.

My teenage years were really hard. I was bullied at school and didn't have many friends. I felt myself losing my native language and I didn't have any Indian friends. I grew closer to my dad, and my brother Gabe was closer to my mom. I felt like she treated him differently than she did me and it caused a separation between us. Now we have a much closer connection, but back then I definitely felt like my brother was her favorite.

**Pali:** When my husband and I separated, Daniel was eight and Gabriel was two and a half. I had custody of both boys for several years. As Daniel got older, he had a lot of anger that I was having a hard time dealing with. I've never been much of an authority figure and I felt that Daniel needed the consistent strong male presence of his father. I can't imagine all the attachment issues Daniel was going through. It's understandable that he would perceive the change in residential custody from me to his father as a rejection. Freeman has a large extended family, so he could offer Daniel aunts and uncles, grandparents and cousins—something I didn't have and we felt he needed.

**Daniel**: Now that I'm older, I appreciate how hard it must have been for her to be a single mom with two kids with no nearby relatives. And I craved what my father's family had to offer, which was more attention than she was able to give at that point. Over time, we've come to work things out. Now there's more gratitude than hard feelings, despite the divorce.

After I read Alex Hayley's book *Roots*, I wanted to learn more about my own native culture. Of course, my Africa was India. I wanted to go there and learn about my heritage. I instinctively knew that I'd learn about my identity and feel better about myself.

As I said, my teenage years were a difficult period. I felt like I didn't fit in anywhere and I wasn't proud of who I was. The kids in my school were either black or white and I didn't fit in with either. When my Dad and I flew into New Deli, my eyes were opened. I started feeling good about who I was and where I came from. It was like discovering my past in a time machine.

If you're of a different race than your adoptive parents it's hard to feel secure, especially if you live in an area where no one else looks like you. My healing didn't begin until I went to India and saw millions of people who shared my heritage. My soul felt enriched. My Dad was the one who stood out in the crowd! That was an amusing turn for us. I developed an appreciation for the culture I was raised in and now I'm proud of my skin color

When I was in Calcutta, I got to speak to Mother Theresa. There was a long line waiting to see her, but when the nuns realized I was one of their own, they brought me right in. When I met her, my whole body started to shake. You could feel the energy coming off her, all the love. I clasped my hands in a prayerful attitude and bowed, thanking her from the bottom of my heart for all she had done for me. She looked up at me and said, "You're so tall!" There I was, expecting pearls of wisdom, but somehow it felt like a blessing.

**Pali**: So in a way, Daniel did find his birth mother when he went back to India.

# LI AND PHILLIP WITH ROSE

• • • • • • • • • • • • • • • • •

**Phillip**: Growing up with five siblings and five cousins next door, I always assumed I'd be a parent one day.

**Li**: I may have thought about being a mother when I was a little kid, but when I got older it never was a driving force. After I got divorced from my first husband, though, I started thinking, "Maybe I should have had children." I was in my late thirties, so I just accepted it wasn't going to happen, until Phillip came along. He had to come to terms with the fact that he probably wouldn't have a biological child if he married me. Once he was comfortable with that decision, adoption was the obvious next step. I wouldn't even say it was the next best thing. It was something we both really wanted to do.

**Phillip**: Before we got married, we decided that if Li wasn't pregnant in a year we'd begin the adoption process.

**Li**: We had a friend in her mid-forties who almost died in childbirth, so that also dampened Phillip's enthusiasm for me to give birth.

**Phillip**: Our decision to adopt from China was a natural evolution. Li's Chinese heritage and our friends' good experience adopting there made us never seriously look into domestic adoption.

**Li**: Unlike in the United States and Eastern Europe, there's very little alcohol or drug abuse in China. The main reason those little girls are given up for adoption is because they're not male.

**Phillip**: Traditionally, the son is considered the future welfare of the Chinese family, as well as the keeper of the family name. With the restrictions on family size for population control, the ratio of boys to girls there has really gotten out of hand. By solving one problem, they've created another one. Since it's illegal in China to give up a child because of gender, a system has developed where baby girls are placed in highly visible locations, then passersby bring them to the police station who, in turn, place them with a social service agency.

I never had much invested in passing my genes down through the generations. I just wanted to be a father. We didn't adopt to do anything altruistic. We wanted to raise a family for the same reason anyone else does. The desire to parent is so strong in human nature that it defies rational justification. When people say, "Rosie is so lucky," I know that Li and I are the lucky ones.

One thing that really bothers me is when people ask, "Is she really yours?" I remember one time talking to a friend about being a parent and when I mentioned adoption, she said, "I just want to have my own child." I was sitting there holding Rosie on my lap. I said, "Look at us. How can you think she's not my own child?" I've also had friends say to me, "If I knew my daughter would be like Rosie, I'd go to China and adopt a daughter right now!'

**Li**: Getting there took a lot of drive and commitment. It takes longer than a pregnancy to go through the paperwork and is much more expensive than prenatal care. We used to joke that writing out each check in the adoption process was like a labor pain! The trip itself was absolutely exhausting. We left at midnight on a Friday from LA, which means we had flown in from the east coast the day before. We landed in China on Sunday morning and caught another flight to our final destination. We were immediately put on a bus ride to the hotel. When we finally arrived, we were told we'd be given our baby after lunch. We were so tired and excited, it was impossible to eat a bite. There were eleven children being placed for adoption that day. All we prospective parents were too excited to stay in our hotel rooms, so

we congregated in the hall. When the director of the orphanage came into the hallway holding Rosie, we knew immediately it was her. She was holding the stuffed panda we'd sent her.

The orphanage director's wife was holding baby DeAnna, who became Rose's best friend back in North Carolina. That's how we met our good friends Wayne and Cindy, DeAnna's parents. We've kept up with other couples from that trip, so when Rose grows up she'll be able to talk to other girls from her same orphanage, if she wants to. When I was growing up I was often the only one in the classroom who looked like me. I hated it. Phillip and I will always live in a racially diverse neighborhood, so Rose won't have to experience that kind of isolation. My Chinese immigrant parents named me Betty in hopes of helping me fit into American society. But I knew I would never look like a Betty, so when I was in my twenties, I changed my name to Wei Li. The funny thing is that even though we named our daughter Rose, after my mother, "Rose" is the name my father gave my mom when she came to America. It's still hard for my mom even to pronounce her own name.

**Phillip**: When our daughter was first placed in our arms, she'd lean away from us and gaze solemnly. Then, after a few days of silence, she became inconsolable. The only time she would stop crying was when someone came to the door.

**Li**: She was definitely grieving for everyone and everything familiar in her short life, especially the *amahs* who had cared for her in the orphanage. But after a short time when she wasn't weeping she was starting to laugh and smile. She'd sit on Phillip's lap at dinner and pat his arm. She definitely bonded with him quicker than she did me. I remember crying myself. I was so worried she'd only like Phil and not me!

**Phillip**: I think these kids are often slower to bond with the mothers because they were replacing their *amahs* from the orphanage. The fathers weren't replacing anybody. Even though Rose clearly was fond of the male orphanage director, I doubt he was much involved in the day-to-day childcare, which is how children learn to love and trust. From the instant she was passed over to us, it felt so right, so strangely familiar. It was like falling in love. There was no room for doubt. There she is—your little girl.

**Li**: We're now in the process of adopting another daughter from China. Phillip always wanted to have

another child so Rosie could have a sister.

**Phillip**: Now that I'm an adult I appreciate having siblings more than ever. I talk with mine about our parents and our childhoods in a way that would be impossible to with anyone else. My mom still talks to at least one of her siblings every day.

**Li**: Wanting another child was a slower process for me than for Phillip, but, having decided, I'm as enthusiastic as he is. I'm close to my own brother and I want Rose to have someone in her life that can be there for her even longer than Phillip and I can be. Without my brother's support, I'd be alone right now in making the decisions for my own parents' well-being. At the end of the day, your family is the most important thing. The paperwork is done, so, basically, we're pregnant right now, waiting for our second child. Rose is as excited as we are. She used to carry around three beanie babies named Mama, Baba and Rosie. Now she has one named Baby Sister, too.

# ROSS AND JUANITA
# WITH JORDAN

••••••••••••••••

**Ross**:  We were in our late twenties when we got married and were thinking more about our careers than having children.

**Juanita**:  Even though I always wanted to be a mother, I wanted to be sure I was in a marriage that was going to last before I raised a family. I've been a psychiatric nurse for over fifteen years, specializing in pediatric problems. So when we found out we were infertile, I was nervous about adoption because I worked every day with kids that had serious mental problems. The more I thought about it though, the more I realized that every family, including mine, has some mental illness in their family tree, so no one gets any guarantees when having a baby.

**Ross**:  After trying IVF twice, we thought about other ways to have children. We went to foster care classes and that's when we got a call about Jordan. It was scary, because we'd only been to about four classes and had no idea we'd be able to get a child so soon. He was only three days old and it wasn't like we'd been through nine months of pregnancy, reading every child care book we could get our hands on. I'd never even held a brand new baby. The next day after that phone call we went and brought him home with us. That evening we were all laying in the bed together looking at him, and I thought, "What do we do now?'

**Juanita**:  That same day we had to go out and get everything we'd need for a newborn. My friends at work were happy for us and they gave me a baby shower a few weeks after we'd gotten him home.

**Ross**:  One reason we were able to adopt so quickly is that, while it's not unusual for black families to take in family members, fewer black families adopt outside of their own kin. It's expensive and just not part of our cultural tradition.

**Juanita**: If the agency had called and said they had a beautiful little white baby for us, I'd probably have said "There are plenty of families waiting to adopt such a child. You don't need us.

**Ross**: Jordan has two older half-brothers and his birth mother's contact information is open if we want to find her. Juanita has sent her pictures of Jordan so she can see how he's growing up. Since he'll probably be an only child for us, it's important that he be able to meet his birth family if he wants to.

**Juanita**: He's a handful, but the joy of our life. It's well worth it. Before we had Jordan, we had a dog for over ten years that we treated like our child. Now we laugh at ourselves when we think how crazy we were about our dog. Having a child puts everything in a different perspective. If anyone asks me about adoption, I say, "It's great." Be prepared to be unprepared, but just do it.

CONSIDERING ADOPTION

# BRYAN AND NANCY
# WITH AUBREY AND LOGAN

●●●●●●●●●●●●●●●●●

**Bryan**: When I was nine years old, my parents adopted a little girl. My brothers and I were so excited we were getting a sister that we didn't give a moment's thought to the fact she was adopted.

**Nancy**: His mother was told she shouldn't have any more pregnancies, but, like my family growing up, their expectation was a large family. My mom's one of nine. My dad's one of five. I have forty two cousins on one side of the family alone. When we got married, it never occurred to me that we wouldn't conceive a child. I went through four surgeries and did the heavy duty hormone route— everything short of in vitro—and that was because our insurance didn't cover it. Even though Bryan grew up with an adopted sister, it took a while for us to get comfortable with not having biological children. I needed to let go of the idea of raising children who looked like us and our family members. Once I did, I didn't care what race the child was. I just wanted a baby!

**Bryan**: Even though my adopted sister didn't look like me and my brothers, she fit right in with the personalities in the family. Even so, it took three years of not being able to conceive, before I finally started to get comfortable with the idea of adoption for Nancy and me.

**Nancy**: One thing that scared us was the stories about couples adopting, then having the baby taken away. We feared the heartache that would cause. I was already so disappointed about not being able to become pregnant, I'd be doubly heartbroken if an adoption fell through. The Baby Jessica story was all over the press at the time and those pictures of her being dragged away from the only parents she'd ever known were seared in our brains. Fortunately, we felt comfortable with the adoption service sponsored by our church. At Latter Day Saints Family Services, the birth mothers choose the adoptive family for their child after reading their applications. We waited for two years before we got the call that a baby boy had been born and we'd been chosen by his birth mother. We've never been so excited in our lives as we were when we drove to the hospital. He was sound asleep when they placed him in our arms. He opened his eyes and looked at us like, "Yep, you guys will work." Then he conked out again. He felt like ours the minute we held him. Of course, on the way home from the hospital, we had to stop by all the relatives and show him off. It was after midnight when we got home, and both Bryan and Logan went right to sleep. I think I stayed awake all night, just staring at him. All the suffering over my infertility just vanished. I was a mother, and it felt so good.

It's funny to think that I used to say I'd never complain about any of the challenges of motherhood if I was able to adopt. I've come to learn that part of being a normal, healthy parent is to talk things through with friends and family. It's OK to say you're tired if a sick child has kept you up three nights in a row.

**Bryan**: The agency only allows two infant adoptions a family so as soon as we could, we applied again for another baby. Once again we had to wait a couple of years before we got Aubrey. We got a call that Logan's birth mother was pregnant again, and she wanted us to adopt this baby as well. Through ultrasound during her pregnancy, the doctors discovered that Aubrey had a heart defect. Although we never considered adopting a sick or handicapped baby, the minute we heard about her, she was ours. Even though the doctors were painting a pretty bleak picture, I always felt that she would be alright. I felt like she was our baby from the moment I knew she was on the way, and that we could face any challenge and make things right.

**Nancy**: She had a defective valve and a hole in her heart, but it was repairable. She was kept on oxygen off and on until she had corrective surgery at four. Valentine's Day seemed like a good date for open heart surgery. She bounced right back and has been on the move ever since. These kids remind us so much of ourselves. Aubrey's more like me, always busy. Whereas, Logan is more reserved like his dad.

**Bryan**: Logan is quite like me. We can sit in our little corners and get lost in our projects for hours. Genealogy is more than a hobby for Mormons, because we believe we can and should seal not only our biological and adopted children to us for all eternity, but our deceased ancestors as well.

**Nancy**: Even though two kids is a small family for people in our church, our kid's favorite word is cousins. They are close to all of their aunt's and uncle's children. What's really funny about our initial hesitation to adopt is, when you look at both sides of our families, we've got diabetes, ADHD, you name it. Our genes aren't any better than anyone else's. No one knows what they're getting when they have a baby, whether they give birth or adopt.

PART FOUR:

OPEN AND CLOSED
ADOPTIONS

# GRETCHEN AND JAY WITH LILY AND MOLLY

**Gretchen**: We knew when we married that we wanted to raise a family. Unlike some couples who go through years of trying to conceive, we understood pretty quickly that I wouldn't be able to get pregnant. After several years of marriage, we felt settled enough to begin the adoption process.

**Jay**: My sister and I were adopted, so I knew it was a good option for creating a family. I had no angst because it had been a loving experience for me. We contacted the same private agency that had placed me and my sister with our adoptive parents.

**Gretchen**: Neither of us were comfortable with the way they operated. It seemed elitist. They specialized in blond, blue-eyed WASP infants. It didn't feel right to be working with people who didn't share our values.

**Jay**: At that time, the agency wouldn't even accept babies of ethnic origin. It all felt a bit creepy—like a throwback to a time and place we didn't want to be.

**Gretchen**: So we contacted social services and started working with them. At the same time I needed to do something pro-active. I knew it could be at least two or three years before a baby became available. So I wrote letters to colleges and women's support groups about ourselves and our desire to adopt. One of those letters got passed on to the person who became Lily and Molly's birth mother. In April she contacted us and said that she'd selected us as her unborn baby's parents. She thought she was due mid-May but by early June we still hadn't heard back from her. We didn't know how to get in touch because she didn't have a telephone.

Meanwhile we got a call from social services saying that they had a baby for us locally. One of my strongest beliefs is that kids end up where God intends them to be. So we said "no" to social services, because we still believed that our baby would be given to us by her birth mother. Soon after, we got a call from her in New Hampshire that Lily had arrived. So just twenty four hours after she was born we went there to get her. The little boy that we were offered by social services actually ended up in the same day care program as Lily! It was obvious that he belonged with his adoptive family just as Lily belonged with us. Lily's

> **One of my strongest beliefs is that kids end up where God intends them to be. —Gretchen**

birth mom had planned out just how she was going to hand her daughter over to us. We all left the hospital together and she placed this perfect little girl in my arms. We have pictures of that moment. And we made an agreement that we'd send her pictures from time to time as Lily grew up.

About two years later we got another call from Lily's birth parents, saying that she was pregnant again and they weren't able to take on another child. They were already raising Lily's older sister and were still desperately poor teenagers, living with her mother. But a few months later she called and said that they decided to keep this baby and have her tubes tied after she delivered.

After that disappointment we tried to adopt another child locally, but the birth mother changed her mind right after the birth. We already had a nursery set up and Lily was excited about a new baby sister. She might have been a lot more upset but the same day that we found out about the birth mother's decision, we picked up Lily's baby doll from the repair shop. She was so delighted to get her doll back that she considered that her new baby sister.

**Jay:** That nursery was taken apart in about half an hour. Our biggest concern was what it was going to do to Lily. When it became apparent that she was content to get her doll back, we just accepted the situation.

**Gretchen:** I'd decided that if we didn't get another child by the time I was thirty five, then Lily would be an only child. About a year later we got a phone call from Lily's birth mother. She was pregnant again. The doctor who delivered her son had had a heart attack in the delivery room, and, in the confusion, she didn't get her tubes tied. Once again, fate intervened and Molly was meant to be. Her birth mom was very clear, very convincing, that this time she wasn't going to change her mind. On January 2, we got a call from her in New Hampshire that Molly had arrived. We brought Lily with us and she held her new baby sister in the hospital.

**Lily:** I remember when we went to get Molly, all of us lining up on a couch to have our picture taken. I didn't really realize at the time that I was with my other brother and sister.

**Jay:** In the four and a half years since we'd adopted Lily, the laws had changed quite a bit to protect birth mothers from being coerced into relinquishing their babies. Now, the birth parents had to appear in the Virginia court with lawyers for both the parents and the infant. It was a very moving experience. The girls' birth parents didn't even own a car, but they somehow made the long trip to get down here. They seemed as grateful as we were to finalize the adoption. Everyone was in tears. Not only the parents, but even the judge, the bailiff and the social worker were in tears.

**Gretchen:** I think it helped the birth parents to feel closure to see where we lived and how their two daughters were thriving. They knew their daughters would have more opportunities here than if they had kept them. Even though they'd gotten married, they were still in no financial situation to raise four kids. We've told the girls that when they're eighteen we'd be happy to help them meet their biological family.

**Molly**: Hey, I'm nineteen! I'm ready when you are! But seriously, even though I'm interested, it's not like some burning desire. Maybe it's because I know that they're not hidden or a mystery. I just assume I'll meet them one day. Like my dad, being adopted is something I'm very comfortable with. It doesn't seem like a big deal.

When I was in sixth or seventh grade, my girlfriends would sometimes be curious about my being adopted. It's not like, "Hi, I'm Molly. I'm adopted," but it's not a big secret either.

**Gretchen**: They know that their birth parents made the decision to have them adopted out of love for them. It wasn't a reckless or irresponsible decision. They only thought about what was best for these two girls.

**Lily**: Hey, Mom! Tell the story about our biological grandfather when Molly was born.

**Gretchen**: I'd forgotten about that. You've got a better memory than I do. Okay, the night before we went to pick up Molly, we got a call from her birth father, who said that his own father—who had abandoned him as a child—wanted custody of Molly. He said he was under a lot of pressure, but had insisted that he wanted Molly to live with us and Lily.

**Jay**: The girls' biological parents were still living in this small place of her mother's. They knew how sparse their financial and emotional resources were. So they chose to give their unplanned baby a good life with two loving parents who could give her a future with better possibilities. If you look at the four of us together, you can tell we're a family.

**Molly**: When I have a family, I'll probably adopt. Why make another baby when there are so many already born that need good homes?

**Lily**: Well, I feel like I'm in the right place at the right time. And I know Molly does too.

**Gretchen**: That's grand praise, especially coming from teenagers. When I was a teenager I used to think, "I couldn't possibly be related to this family! I must be adopted!'

# JERRY WITH A PHOTOGRAPH OF HER TWIN SISTER AND ADOPTIVE MOTHER

• • • • • • • • • • • • • • • •

My parents divorced when my twin sister and I were eighteen. Twenty years later, when Daddy was divorcing his second wife, she discovered our adoption papers. She took it upon herself to call my sister Judy and give her the unexpected news. The first thing Judy did was call me and ask if I knew that we were adopted. Of course I was as surprised as she was—shocked, really. Discovering in middle age that you're adopted is like having the rug pulled out from under you. You're suddenly sprawled on the floor going, "Huh?" When we called our mother, she wouldn't break the promise of secrecy she'd made to our father. She'd only say, "I have to talk to your father about this."

The three of us all made the trip to Roanoke to discuss our discovery with Daddy. When I confronted him about the secrecy, he said he'd been afraid we wouldn't love him as much if we knew the truth. Our parents told us that our birth mother had eight previous children before she gave birth to my sister and me. Ten children was more than she could feed, so we were given to the state to be put up for adoption. Mama and Daddy had been married for twelve years without ever getting pregnant, so they adopted us. When we were about eight years old, they were discussing telling us about being adopted when Mama got pregnant with our first brother, Bobby. Then they were afraid that we'd be insecure if we knew they weren't our biological parents. Three years later she gave birth to Tommy and they considered their secret was permanently sealed from us.

Everybody in our little town knew we were adopted, except us four kids. I don't think our neighbors knew it was a big secret within our family. They just assumed we all knew so there was nothing to discuss. The shocking news wasn't as big a deal to our younger brothers. One of them, "You're still my sister, the same girl who used to beat us up all the time when we were kids!"

My sister Judy took the news of being adopted really hard. She was always a drinker, but she really hit the bottle after she found out we were adopted. Later,

> **Discovering in middle age that you're adopted is like having the rug pulled out from under you. You're suddenly sprawled on the floor going, "Huh?" —Jerry**

when Daddy died, she spun out of control and within a few years was dead too, from alcohol poisoning. She was trying to drown out the pain of an abusive childhood.

I still have large gaps in my memory of when we were young. I was definitely the black sheep, so I got more than my share of physical and verbal abuse. It turns out, though, that I was the lucky one. My sister didn't get whipped or yelled at as much as I did, but Daddy took advantage of Judy's timid nature and sexually abused her over the years. My relationship with him was one big argument. When Judy and I moved out of the house at eighteen, Daddy left Mama. He was definitely hanging around for his adopted daughter, Judy, more than for our mother.

I always felt responsible for Judy and she always felt responsible for Daddy. She was the one who took care of him when he got old. If he'd been molesting me, I don't even want to think what I'd have done to him. That's probably why he left me alone. He had a power over her that I could never understand.

When Daddy died, Judy didn't live long. Once we discovered we had a biological family out there somewhere, Daddy started telling Judy all kinds of terrible things about her birth mother, so she would be afraid to meet her. Sometimes he told her she was dead. I never believed a word out of that man's mouth, but my sister hung on to everything he said. Because of Daddy's stories, she had this image in her mind of an old station wagon

loaded down with dirty, raggedy kids, an old man with no teeth and tobacco juice in his beard, and an illiterate hag showing up on our doorstep one day. Daddy didn't want to lose the power he had over Judy, so he scared her to death about her birth parents.

Now that Judy, Mama, and Daddy have died, I'm working with a company called Omnitrace to get information about my biological parents. I'm hoping one or the other is fat, so I can understand my chunky build. I look like nobody in my family, not even my biological twin sister! My two brothers are my father's spitting image—walking carbon copies of him. Even Judy favored our mother more than I did. I never had a baby, so evidently I didn't inherit my birth mother's baby-making ability! Judy had one child, who is as interested as me in finding out more about those secret relatives. My niece is a lot more like me than her mama. There's not a timid bone in her body. My father couldn't stand her. All he ever had were complaints about his granddaughter, Leigh Ann, He didn't like either one of us because we weren't under his control like Judy was. Leigh Ann would sometimes say to me, "I wish he liked me more'. I'd say, "Oh no you don't! You don't need to go there!" Leigh Ann and I have always been very close. Besides my sister who died, she's the only blood relative I've ever known.

About two months ago, Leigh Ann and I went over to the county where her mom and I were born to search through

the records. It's not easy to unravel a closed adoption that took place fifty years ago. But Omnitrace says they can probably come up with some answers to our questions. After Daddy passed away, we found some adoption papers that had fallen behind his dresser that had our birth mother's name on it. Judy wanted to destroy the paper, but I wouldn't let her. Even if my birth parents have died, I almost certainly have some biological brothers and sisters out there.

As much as I disliked Daddy's second wife, I think she did me a favor by telling the truth about our background.

Daddy died of heart failure after years of heart disease and Mama died of cancer, but since I'm no blood relation, I don't have those genes. At least it makes me less fearful about my health. On the other hand, my doctor told me that one of my close relations must have been an alcoholic and that Judy's fate was genetic. My search for my birth family isn't because I don't consider the family that raised me my "real family." As for my brothers, I feel as close to them as any sister could. It would be nice, though, to know about the people who are my closest blood kin. Not to reject my family, but to know more about myself.

PART FIVE:

SINGLE PARENT
ADOPTION

# JULIE WITH CHRIS AND HOLLY

•••••••••••••••••

I'd heard of a "call" to enter the ministry, but didn't believe it existed until it happened to me. A friend first planted the idea in my head but I didn't take it seriously. A week later, when I made myself consider it, it was like being hit with a cannonball that had two thousand years of momentum. God wanted all of my attention, not just Sunday morning. I've been an ordained priest in the Episcopal Church for twenty three years now.

It never occurred to me to have children unless I was married, but after seven or eight years in ministry, God spoke to me again and said "adopt a child". I'm not talking about a hunch or an idea, I'm talking about a revelation from which there is no arguing. The very next day I got out the yellow pages and looked up adoption agencies. I was too old, didn't have much money and I was single, but I was operating on instructions from divine inspiration and didn't listen to the people who told me I was on a hopeless quest.

Several agencies did reject my application and I had some heartbreaking disappointments before I finally became a mother. Once, after I was told by an agency that they had a baby for me, I got a call during my baby shower saying it had fallen through. All eyes were on me, waiting for me to tell them the time and place where I was to get my baby. Instead, I shut the door to the nursery and cried. Eventually I got a call at 5:00 AM from an adoption agency in Brazil. They said that a baby girl was waiting for me if I could get down there with $9000 cash in one week. The most amazing thing is when I went to withdraw my money from my savings account, the teller told me I had enough money in my checking account to withdraw the amount I needed. I knew I had very little money in that account, but somehow everything I needed was there. I just withdrew the $9000 and thanked God. A minor miracle, but a miracle none the less. I ironed the ninety $100 bills and loaded them into two money belts.

The Brazilian agency instructed me to bring clock radios, so I got a huge suitcase from a yard sale and filled it with diapers and clock radios. Ironing hundred dollar bills and filling suitcases with clock radios is not the way most women prepare for motherhood, but we each have our own path. From the pulpit Sunday morning,

I told my congregation that I was leaving the next morning for Brazil.

After flying all night, I missed my connecting flight in Rio. By some miracle, my luggage stayed behind with me. I was so afraid I'd never see it again because I knew that where I was going, there would be nothing to buy, especially baby supplies. Murphy's Law must have been invented in Brazil. Nothing worked—the phones, the airline schedules, everything—was conditional at best.

After a four hour wait in line, I got access to a working phone and contacted the adoption agency about my indefinite delay. There were labor strikes at the airlines and everything was at a standstill. In line, I told a flight attendant about my upcoming adoption and she gave me a flight attendant pass so I could get on the next plane. I finally made my way to the agency and was given directions to get to the little town where Holly was born. Once I got there, this lawyer showed up with a tiny baby who was wearing nothing but a pair of running shorts that would fit a four year old. Those shorts were Holly's only earthly possession. She was born in a house with no address that you couldn't get to by car and she lived in an orphanage with a dirt floor and no running water.

I handed over the money and the lawyer handed over the baby. He counted out the $100 bills on the bed while the baby slept next to me. A hundred dollars went to the orphanage and the rest went to the attorneys, judges and assorted bureaucrats that clog the efficiency of every transaction that takes place in that country. Then I handed out clock radios to every transcriber, translator and clerk of the court that I had dealt with on my path to becoming a mother. When they first placed Holly in my arms and I was walking up the hotel stairs to my room, I wondered how long it would take until I felt like she was my daughter. By the time I got to the top of the stairs, she was mine.

The hardest part was that I had Holly for four days and the judge still wouldn't sign the release papers because he didn't like Americans taking South American children out of the country. After he was sure I'd missed my flights, he released her to me. By now I'd been there for ten days and had run out of everything—diapers, formula, money, even radio alarm clocks! I was up for forty eight hours going from airport to airport until I finally got a seat on a departing plane to Rio. In Rio I stood in line from 6:30 in the morning until 5:50 in the evening to get Holly's visa. Then, when all the paperwork was finally completed, I bought a book about the region where Holly was born before heading to our final flight home. The line at immigration to get her green card was no better when I arrived in the States. Through all of this, Holly was an angel, sweetly sleeping or smiling through most of it. That's her disposition to this day.

I'd thought all along that I didn't want to have an only child. Because I'm an older single parent, I felt two kids could give each other more support than I could offer by myself. The social workers knew from the beginning that I was looking to adopt a second child. When Holly was twenty two months old, I got a call about Chris. I had twenty four hours to accept before they continued down the list of thirty six waiting families. I gave a tentative "yes," then checked in with the Lord. There was no reply—nothing but silence. Even so, years before I ever thought of having children, I had dreamed I had a son who was patting me softly and his name was Chris. So I accepted the offer, because of the dream, and because I was afraid if I said "no" it would hurt my chances of getting another opportunity.

The social worker said Chris had a "few medical problems," but I didn't have the sense to go into what they were. It turned out he was a crack cocaine baby. He was in the

hospital with terrible withdrawal for two weeks after he was born, then in a foster home for a week. I picked him up when he was three weeks old and he screamed in the car seat the entire ride home. He didn't stop for a year. I don't think I would have had the strength to keep him if I hadn't told Holly that this was her new brother and that he'd be part of our family forever. Eventually I was afraid to drive, because sleep deprivation was making me hallucinate. The poor baby screamed night and day, kicking so frantically that his tiny feet were bloody. It took me much longer to bond with him than it did with Holly, because he couldn't even make eye contact, much less smile. He didn't even sit up for ten months and I eventually had to teach him to crawl. I'd put Cheerios on the floor in front of him and move his arms and legs for him until he got them.

When it was time to walk, I wouldn't let him crawl. I'd make him walk to his Cheerios. After he started walking,

I had to put a screen over his crib so he couldn't get out. Otherwise, he'd be roaming through the house all night, getting into trouble. He had no instincts for self-preservation. For years, it seemed like he tripped on thin air and was constantly bruised. When he started school, his teachers were always calling me to report some accident. It took him so much longer to learn anything. His first grade teacher told me she doubted he'd ever read.

Today he's an honor student with a wonderful sense of humor and such an athlete, he won the Presidential Award for physical fitness, as well as the only trophy awarded a seventh grader for soccer. He and Holly are very protective of and devoted to each other and they are so considerate towards me. It was a long time coming to get to this place, but what a journey—what a wonderful thing. Even though we don't look anything alike, Holly and I are so alike that it's hard to imagine having a biological child who could be any more similar. Chris needed someone who believed in his ability to succeed and I needed him to teach me patience.

There are wonderful parallels between God's love and a parent's love. Loving my children has made me feel even closer to God. In our church, we say we are the adopted children, the heirs of Christ. I have a different understanding of that concept after all I've experienced raising my daughter and son. God accepts us unconditionally, just as we love our children. Being a mother has made me much more sensitive towards my congregation. My children have made me more authentic, in a way that no degree or career success ever could. They've expanded the depth and breadth of my humanity.

# NELLY
# WITH ADRIANA

••••••••••••••••

I'm a single mother and was divorced many years ago. By the time I was in my mid-forties, I realized I wasn't going to be a mother unless I adopted. Motherhood was something I didn't want to miss. Having emigrated from Cuba with my Spanish parents, you'd think I'd want to go to a Latin American country and get a Latino child. But I'd heard so many horror stories about people traveling great distances and spending a great deal of money, only to have the adoption fall through. A friend had a wonderful experience adopting in China, so since I wasn't getting any younger, I decided to go there myself.

My friends and family were either very quiet about the idea, or just came right out and questioned my sanity. But once Adriana was in my arms, everyone came around with great enthusiasm. Now when I look back and think of traveling half way around the world all by myself, without any idea of how to care for a baby, I think they were right. I might have been a little bit crazy—but I'm so glad I was! On the way over there, I'm sure I looked strange going through the airports with a stroller, diaper bag and teddy bear, but no baby. At the hotel in China they handed me Adriana and said, "Here she is!" She just stared at me with these bright dark eyes and I can see her analyzing the situation. I restrained myself from smothering her with hugs and kisses, because I didn't want her to feel overwhelmed. She didn't seem very impressed with the bear I'd carried in my arms for thousands of miles, but when I offered her a key ring with colorful plastic keys, she hung on for dear life, like it was her security blanket. The next day when the director of the orphanage came by to check on us, Adriana hung on to my neck like she did those keys. I knew she was my daughter.

She's a really focused and curious little girl—always asking a lot of questions. Her favorite expression is "What if…?" She's always known she was adopted from China, but says I'm the only mother she loves because I'm the only one she's known. She does wonder sometimes if she has any Chinese brothers or sisters. She writes stories about twin sisters who discover each other when they're older. Being an immigrant myself, I'm raising her with the assumption of graduate school and a career. But her play centers on being a mother. She has baby dolls of all races but her favorites are the Caucasian ones. I send her to Chinese school every Saturday. She can make the characters beautifully.

Being a single mother strains your resources. There's no one else around to pitch in. My mother used to help out more but she's getting up in years. Now, I'm more looking out for her. When my father died, having Adriana in the family helped both my mother and me so much. She gave us something positive to focus on. Having children can keep you from giving in to grief, because they keep you too busy to indulge your sorrow.

Being a mother has made me much more understanding in my work as a counselor in the public school system. I've always been a patient person. That's why I ended up working with children. But the constant care that a young child demands transforms you into an even more sensitive and sympathetic person.

# MICHELLE WITH
# KATERINA AND ANYA

● ● ● ● ● ● ● ● ● ● ● ● ● ● ● ●

I've always been fascinated with all things Russian. My church had an outreach program to write letters to Russian ministers who were imprisoned before the Iron Curtain fell, and I studied Russian history when I was at U.C. Berkeley. I've been studying the Russian language for the past few years. One of the reasons we're moving to St. Petersburg while I work on my doctorate in civic education is so I can really learn the language. I want my girls to be fluent as well. It's part of their heritage, and now it's part of mine. My intention in adopting them was never to pull them completely away from their roots, but to assimilate their background into their future.

I went on several mission trips to the former Soviet Republic of Kazakhstan with my church group and fell in love with the warmhearted people. I wanted to do more to help than just teach their educators English. But how do you help an entire country? When I went to the orphanages and saw all the babies there who needed homes, I knew that adoption was the most direct way for me to make a real difference in someone's life. I'd always had very traditional expectations—a husband, 2.5 kids, and a dog in a yard with a white picket fence. But that wasn't happening for me. I didn't want to wait indefinitely to have the chance to do something good for a child.

At first my parents were shocked when I told them I was considering single motherhood, but they came to see my adoption plans as a way to serve God. I had so much love to give, while children were just wasting away untouched in orphanage cribs. I personally didn't believe that bringing another child into the world was an option for me, since I'm unmarried. So I took responsibility for ones who were already here and needed a mother. My dream is to open an orphanage in Russia someday. I can never forget all those little babies that are still over there, waiting for homes. So many older children are left behind and I'd like to establish a place where the hard-to-place children could grow up in a loving, nurturing environment.

I got so much encouragement when I went on the internet and read other people's adoption stories. The group Families of Russian and Ukrainian Adoption (FRUA) put me in touch with other families, too. There's a large circle of support around the whole adoption process if you know how to find it. I love talking to people who are interested in going abroad and doing the same thing I did. I love getting those calls, "So and so said you've adopted and we're thinking about it." I don't know if I would have had the courage to adopt if I hadn't been able to see on the internet all the wonderful testimonies of other single moms who've adopted.

Adopting my two girls wasn't easy. It took persistence and faith to see it through. But nothing I've ever done has been more worthwhile. I had to stay in Kazakhstan for six weeks to get through the red tape. I had to get right in front of people who were in charge and show them that I was a mother, not just a name on a piece of paper. By the time I left, the whole town knew about this red headed woman who wouldn't take "no" for an answer!

When I finally got Katerina home, she was eleven months old and the back of her head was flat from having laid in a crib for months without ever being handled. There aren't enough caregivers at the Orphanage to do more than give them a bottle in their crib and change them. At almost a year she couldn't even sit or crawl because she'd never had the chance to learn. Once she got the opportunity

to move around, she caught up pretty quickly, physically. But even years later we're still facing the ramifications of the deprivations she had during her first year of life. Her ability to learn and her motor coordination are still behind her age group because of the sensory deprivation she experienced all those months in a crib.

When Katerina was three, we went to Ukraine together to adopt Anya. Again, it took six weeks there, dealing with the bureaucracy, to find a sister for Katerina. When we did finally find her, she came walking and talking into the waiting room. At sixteen months old, she would mostly just repeat "dye, dye"—Russian for "give me, give me." Growing up in an orphanage, she'd needed those words to get her fair share. The word "Mama" didn't have any meaning until I taught her. Because Anya was older than Katerina when she was adopted, she has more attachment issues because she didn't have a mother figure during the time when those bonds are usually established. She'd go to a stranger as easily as she'd come to me, because she missed that first year and a half of attachment. We're still working on growing that intimate bond. It's something you'd take for granted if you nurtured a baby from infancy, but, in its absence you learn what a significant building block of emotional and social development it is.

Persevering through these developmental obstacles has made us stronger as a family. I don't take anything for

granted. Being a Mother is the greatest gift God has ever given me but it's also a huge responsibility. I know that moving to Russia will be hard for both me and the girls, but it will be worth the effort. Struggle can strengthen your faith and your relationship with each other. Our family will grow closer to each other and to God. That adventure will become part of our family story because that's how you build a family—through shared experience.

# FLORENCE WITH HARRISON AND OCTAVIA

•••••••••••••••••

Like most little girls, I always assumed that I'd have a baby when I grew up. My mother died tragically when I was young and I never had a role model for motherhood. I now realize that my own mother had been miserable as a stay-at-home housewife. But back in the fifties, that was simply what one did. There weren't many options.

I married quite young but that marriage was a bad idea, and we didn't have children together. After the divorce, I left England at twenty eight to come to America and re-invent myself both professionally and personally. I left the music business, became an art director, and met my second husband, who is a photographer. Again, no children. We did the entire run of fertility treatments, including IVF. The whole thing was an awful, heartbreaking ordeal. When I look back on it, I'm amazed at how crazed I was to get pregnant. We could conceive in vitro, but the fertilized eggs wouldn't implant in my womb. Our doctor finally suggested that we find a surrogate to carry our embryo. My husband asked his sister if she'd carry our child for us, and, miraculously, she agreed. Physically, she's the one who gave birth to Harrison, but she's his aunt, not his mother. With the divorce, I guess she is now my ex-sister-in-law, but we'll always be very, very close. I'll be eternally grateful for her generosity. My son wouldn't be here without her.

Both Harrison and Octavia have always known the circumstances of their birth. I don't understand how you can wait and then one day decide, "Well, today's the day to tell them about their birth mother." Harrison has always known he grew inside his aunt and Octavia knows she has birth parents in China, but we are her Mommy and Daddy. She likes to tell this story she made up about being in China. She's crying—waiting for Mommy and Daddy to come get her. Then we come and get her and that's the end of the story. It's her own personal fairy tale.

I can clearly remember a specific moment—I was out shopping with my own sister after Harrison was born—when I realized how important it was to me that

Harrison have a sibling. I wanted him to have that lifelong bond with another human being. I knew a woman who had adopted a little girl from China and told me about a group called World Association for Children and Parents. Because of ancient patriarchal traditions and contemporary population control policies, China was full of little girls without parents. Since there are so many couples in the West who are longing to build a family, it just makes sense to put the two together. It took about a year from the time we started the paper work until we flew over there to bring Octavia home. After you apply with the agency and send them a huge dossier with all your pertinent information, you just wait. One day you get a tiny little picture, like the one on your passport, and a brief medical report. You have to decide almost immediately whether you're going to make the trip and bring her home. It's totally irrational, but you fall in love with that little photograph.

We traveled there with two other families and, magically, none of us had any doubt that we all got the right child. When we first brought Octavia back to the hotel room for a nap, I looked at this sleeping baby and realized that when she wakes up she's going to be with total strangers and hear English for the first time. When she woke up, she looked at me and I said, "Octavia, I think we should go find Daddy and Harrison and get some lunch." I got

her dressed, put her on my hip and carried her downstairs like we'd been doing it her entire life. We had our first lunch together as a family of four. Because Harrison was with us, I don't think having a baby sister was as big an adjustment for him. His Mommy didn't disappear into a hospital and return after days of separation with a new baby.

These two kids are total opposite personalities. Harrison is so easygoing and undemanding, and Octavia is so flamboyant and in your face. The two of them make a perfect team.

I always continued working, even with two small children, as my career made more income than my husband's. The increased physical and emotional demands of two young children in New York City pushed our marriage to the breaking point. My husband was, and is, a wonderful, playful and attentive father, but I got tired of feeling like I was the only grownup in the household. I felt like I was taking care of everybody all the time and the resentment spoiled the relationship. I just couldn't stand to wake up mad every day. I'd rather be alone, which I am. But I'd never say for one minute that it was all my ex-husband's fault that we got divorced. It takes two to muck it up. The divorce was not the kids fault. Our relationship just couldn't rise to the occasion.

CONSIDERING ADOPTION

Since my mother's suicide when I was thirteen, I'd always been extremely competent and self-sufficient. To a fault, actually. I wouldn't allow myself to be too dependent on anyone else for my happiness. I realize now that that was a weakness instead of a strength.

My kids are the light of my life. They've taught me about unconditional love and given my life more meaning. Even my work means more to me, because I'm providing for them as well as myself.

# PART SIX:

## ADOPTING
## MANY CHILDREN

# STEVEN AND JEAN WITH ANNE MARIE, JON MATTHEW, CHRISTIAN, JOSEPH, VICTORIA, NICHOLAS, THOMAS, MARY KATHRYN, BENJAMIN, ANA GABRIEL, AND SARAH ELIZABETH

••••••••••••••••••

**Jean**:  After our first two sons, Jared and Jacob were born, I couldn't have more children. Since we knew we wanted a large family, we began the adoption process. It took us ten years to adopt our first, but soon after we adopted Anne Marie, we got Jon Matthew six weeks later. They were raised like twins. Joseph came next. He was such a quiet baby, not nearly the active handful that Anne Marie and Jon were.

When the stories about the Rumanian orphanages hit the news, my sister-in-law and I were so moved by their dire situation that we decided to go over there and adopt. We were there for five weeks while Steven stayed home with the other kids. The poverty at the orphanage was heart wrenching. As I was in the process of adopting Christian and Victoria, the twins, Nicholas and Thomas, were born and placed in the orphanage. One baby was so sick, he had a fever of one hundred and seven degrees. The staff at the orphanage knew he'd never survive unless he got medical care outside of Romania. He had pneumonia and hepatitis. I felt like I couldn't just abandon them there to die. Christian tested positive for AIDS, but it turned out they'd gotten the blood work switched in the lab. He was completely malnourished and at four, wasn't even walking yet.

**Steven**:  Hearing about all this long distance, I figured I'd better fly over there and see what was going on. We were doubling the size of our already large family overnight! We didn't even have a car big enough to pick up four new kids at the airport! Our family and friends just rolled their eyes and laughed, "That's Jean for you," they'd say. "She never does anything halfway." I have to admit, Jean has a lot more energy than I do. Bringing all these kids into our family was definitely not my idea. They owe their good fortune to their mother.

> **What I love about our family is that all of us adopted kids feel special, and wanted. Our parents went through a lot of effort to get us before they even started the work of raising us. —Jon Matthew**

**Jean**: Steven was never a complainer. I always had his love and support. He can cook, clean and take care of the kids as well as, if not better than, I can. That first year when we had the four new kids from Romania was overwhelming. We could never have done it if we weren't on each other's side.

**Steven**: It got really crazy after Jean got back from Romania with four new children. We were in a home with room for four kids, not ten. We had mattresses on the floor. The twins were under the grand piano in a basket. One evening when we came home, our two oldest sons, who were teenagers at the time, told us there was a lady from social services at the house, checking out the accommodations. They said she seemed really mad. They finally took pity on our panic and said, "April Fools!" And, in fact, it was April first. We really needed a sense of humor during that time in our lives.

**Jean**: Six years later, I began to feel like there were still children yet to come to us. Steven thought ten kids was plenty, plus we were living in an even smaller house while we were building the one we're in today. This time I went through an adoption facilitator in California and we got Ben. At the time, Steven was less than enthused by my determination so its poetic justice that today Ben and Steven are joined at the hip. Ben would be the first to tell you his best friend is his dad.

**Steven**: So we weren't not surprised when, of course, we adopted another child after Ben. Jean didn't want him to feel like an only child with the six year age gap between him and his brothers and sisters.

**Jean**: Anna Gabriella came a year later.

**Steven**: And as if that wasn't enough, soon after that we got a call from Benjamin's birth mom. She was pregnant again and she wanted this baby to be with her brother. We really didn't feel like there was a choice to be made. Sarah Elizabeth was part of the family as soon as she was born.

**Jean**: We feel strongly that this family is meant to be together. To me, thirteen is a lucky number. Each of the kids knows their own unique birth story. And being one of so many adopted kids, no one feels left out or lesser for not being blood relatives.

**Jon Matthew**: What I love about our family is that all of us adopted kids feel special and wanted. Our parents went through a lot of effort to get us before they even started the work of raising us.

**Jean**: Our two older boys have been so supportive. Whenever they call or write home, the first thing they say is how much they miss the kids. No one in this family feels out of place. We're a great fit.

# MICHAEL WITH HIS MOTHER, NANCY

●●●●●●●●●●●●●●●

*(Speaking at her home in a retirement community, before being joined by her son, Michael.)*

**Nancy**: I was married at eighteen and my oldest daughter was born a year later. My husband was in the military. Over the next sixteen years we had four girls and two boys. Our prime interest was children. After he got out of the military he was a YMCA executive and I was a preschool teacher. When our youngest son was seven, a dear friend of ours died and we wanted to do something worthwhile in his memory. I learned about the Indian Adoption Project and we adopted our son, Andrew, who's an Apache, when he was fourteen months old. When he was two, he needed a brother closer in age than his big brothers, so we adopted Mike when he was seven months old. By that time, our four girls were off at school and our two boys thought it was great to have more kids in the family.

Andrew was always quiet, not in a withdrawn way, but almost stern. It was hard on him that he looked different than his family and schoolmates. Once, we took him to see a group of Indian children doing traditional tribal dances. The North East Indian tribes here have been so inter-married though the generations that they looked like all the other Caucasian kids. Even though Andrew was one of the spectators, everyone gathered around him because he looked like an Indians like on TV or in the movies.

Mike never even noticed that he was black until he went to school. While Andrew dealt with his differentness by being aggressive, Mike was always a lover instead of a fighter. He was such an open and affectionate child that he won people over immediately.

When Mike was six we adopted a fourteen year old mixed race black Korean boy. He came to us speaking only a few words of English. My husband and I had started a parent's adoption group called Room For One More and we had the books from the Holt International Adoption Agency. The books had pictures and descriptions of all the kids who needed families. I kept being drawn to one boy's picture until it became obvious that he belonged here with us. Ken settled in remarkably quickly. He started school right away and picked up English in no time. He had been abandoned at two and lived in an orphanage until his teens, so he had a lot to overcome to feel secure in our home. He joined the military after high school because he wanted to get back to Korea but he's out of the service now and working as a croupier at the Taj Mahal in Atlantic City.

After Ken had settled in, we still had room for one more, so we adopted a little boy from Vietnam. He had been orphaned in the war. No one knew how old he was when he arrived. We guessed about eight. Not surprisingly, Josh had a lot of fears and insecurities from his war-torn childhood. We never knew if his parents were actually killed or if they stuck him on an airlift plane to get him out of harm's way. He's married with two kids of his own now.

Having given birth to six children and adopting four more, I can say with absolute certainty that there was no difference in our feelings for our biological and our adopted children. We are a family of twelve. When we started adopting, interracial adoptions were rare and not encouraged, but we knew there weren't enough families of color to adopt all the kids who needed homes. We really pushed to be able to adopt hard-to-place kids. Success in raising a child of a different race depends on the personality of the child. If you think about it, success in raising a biological child is also dependent on the personality of the child. So the fact is, life is easier for some and harder for others, whether adopted or not. When Mike was a little boy, I asked him why everyone spoke to him. How did he know all those people? He said,

"They all want to know me because I'm black." I said, "Don't you suppose they want to know you because you're a nice guy?" And he said, "Oh, yeah—that too!" He liked everyone and assumed they'd feel the same way. His brother Andrew was quite the opposite growing up.

I'm not sure how we raised ten kids on a YMCA salary, but somehow we always managed. We ran the YMCA summer camp for twenty seven years, so our kids always had the benefit of living the outdoor life. We never felt they needed brand new stuff. There were always ski swap sales and used bikes available.

I have seventeen grandchildren and seven great grandchildren. Many of them are adopted. My oldest son has a daughter from Haiti. My second daughter adopted three children. My third daughter works in adoption and wrote a wonderful book on the subject, *Real Parents, Real Children*. She adopted a daughter from India and a son from Costa Rica. While growing up, our children learned the value of adoption and have shared our philosophy of opening your heart to those in need. We still get together for family camp every summer, even though my husband passed away a year and a half ago. Our family continues to grow but there's always room for one more.

*(Nancy's son, Michael, arrives and joins the conversation.)*

**Michael**: Something unusual about my place in the family is that I'm the youngest, even though two more brothers came after me. I don't think I ever realized how unique my family was until I reached junior high. I thought other families were odd because everyone looked alike. Normal for me was what I experienced in my home every day. Because of my own family, and mom's involvement in Room for One More, I was surrounded by a large population of adopted kids. I looked at adoption as being hand-picked. I felt proud of it, like a glorified entity! Not that I didn't get picked on as a kid. Everyone does. But my dad taught me that a bully is someone who feels bad about himself and is trying to build himself up by bringing you down. Because I knew this at a young age, they couldn't really get to me. I just felt sorry for them.

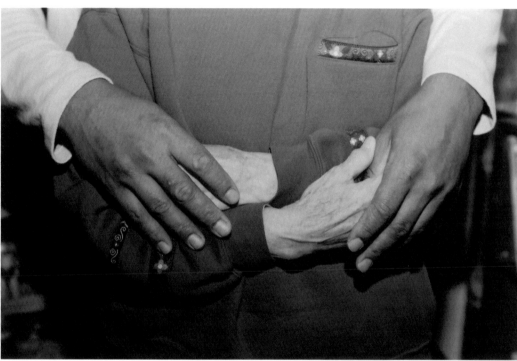

Every day my mom and dad told me that they loved me, and I believed them. It's a great way to grow up. I was proud of being the only kid in school with an Afro. I remember looking in the mirror and thinking, "My nose is wider, my skin is darker, my hair is curlier, but everyone else looks different, too. That's nature's plan, to make no two of us look the same." When I saw identical twins, it seemed strange to me.

Even though the ten of us all have different interests and personalities, there's a bond of sharing the same memories of holidays together and the same day-to-day routine with the same parents that make us a family. Growing up in a large family taught me lessons in patience that help me every day when dealing with other people. I've always enjoyed meeting new people. Like my mom, there always seems to be room for one more in my life. If I'm ever in a position to be a parent, I'll likely adopt. There are so many kids out there who need a home. I've been an uncle since I was two, so in some ways I've been nurturing kids for as long as I can remember!

When I think about my parents adopting four kids after having six of their own, it's amazing. Yet knowing my parents—their love of life and zest for sharing –it makes perfect sense. They nurtured themselves by nurturing others. I've always felt blessed to be adopted by two such loving parents and brought into such a large warm family. Adoption was my second chance, an opportunity to have a better life than my birth parents could have offered. Whoever gave me up for adoption wanted the best for me. It was an act of love more than an act of rejection. My birth mother gave me the gift of an opportunity to be raised by my wonderful adoptive parents. I feel lucky.

# GAIL WITH AARON, SAMANTHA, NOAH, ZACHARY AND LEAH

• • • • • • • • • • • • • • • •

When I was a child I was inspired by Danny Kaye in the old UNICEF public service newsreels in the movie theater. He'd be surrounded by little African and Indian kids with big eyes and distended bellies. As a kid I had this fantasy of marring a rich man and, after having a few kids of our own, traveling around the world adopting babies. The husband never materialized but I didn't let that keep me from pursuing my goals. When I split up with my longtime boyfriend I was in my late thirties and it was my father who encouraged me to consider artificial insemination. Aaron is the result. When he was older, I tried to get pregnant through that route again, but it didn't happen.

I never made it around the world with Danny Kaye so I improvised, especially since it had always been my dream to adopt. I just did it later in life than I had anticipated and I did it alone. Aaron came with me to Philadelphia when we adopted Samantha. She was a scrunched up little thing with a "Fro" bigger than her body. I'm wondering "When will I start feeling like I'm her mother?" Aaron took one look at her and said, "Mom, she's so ugly, I gotta get out of here!" But the next day I mentioned to Aaron that I think Samantha is getting prettier by the minute. He said, "No, Mom. She's getting prettier by the second!"

Three years later, a pregnant birth mother chose me to adopt her baby. She had read my essay "A Day in the Life" that I'd written for my adoption lawyer to show his birth mother clients. After Noah was born, we drove through a snow storm to get him from the hospital. When he was five months old, my son Zachary became available through a friend of the family. We couldn't resist him. Noah and Zachary were raised like twins, sharing everything. So Zach was my surprise pregnancy! I didn't seek him out. He found me.

After I had adopted my first three kids, our social worker suggested that I start my own adoption agency. I laughed, but thirty minutes later decided that was exactly what I was going to do. Since I'm single, I was living on my retirement savings to be a stay-at-home mom. I was running out of money but didn't want to be out of the house all day, so I got a license and opened the Mandala Adoption Agency right here in my home.

Four years after I'd started Mandala, I decided to adopt a girl from China. You can't facilitate your own adoption, so I worked with another agency. At the same time, Aaron was preparing for his bar mitzvah, with a hundred and fifty people coming from out of town for the big day. Of course, as fate would have it, I got a letter from the agency saying that if I wanted to adopt Leah I had to be in China that same weekend. Aaron was coming with me and it didn't seem possible to cancel either event, so we decided to do both! We had our Friday night service, the Saturday morning bar mitzvah and the big party Saturday night. Then, at six o'clock on Sunday morning, he and I were on a plane to China. My two sisters hosted all our out-of-town guests that day for brunch while we flew to the other side of the world. When we finally made it to the orphanage, Aaron was the first to hold Leah. It was definitely worth all the travel to get there, because we got the best kid in the world!

Maybe there was once a time when adoption was considered second best. People might secretly adopt a child that looked like them and then pretend it was their biological baby. Today, many of my clients chose to adopt not because they can't conceive but because they want to offer love to a child that needs it. Open adoptions, where the birth mother chooses the adoptive parents and keeps some ongoing relationship with them after they relinquish their baby, is more and more common. The sigma and shame from adoption is dismantled when there's no secrecy. There's nothing to be secretive about.

At my agency, we love to expand the horizons of people who are interested in adoption. We always ask if they have a racial preference for their adoptive child. No matter what their answer is, we always discuss their reasons in depth. Adopting outside of your race adds another dimension, just like raising a baby who's not biologically related. Both can be positive, but you have to go in with your eyes open. We also question peoples' motives for adoption if they'll only consider a baby that can "pass" for their genetic offspring. One thing we insist on is that the adoptive parents not be secretive with their child about their adoption. We believe that, to the extent possible, it's every child's right to know the history of their beginnings. Secrecy promotes shame. Our first obligation is to the child, even though our source of income is from the parents. A good adoption agency should share knowledge and be a support system as well as facilitate adoptions.

As a facilitator, I might encourage or discourage an adoption, depending on what's best for both the baby and the adoptive parents. Every day I'm grateful for how much I love my job. It's as gratifying as my family life. In some ways, it's like raising my kids, which at times can be almost as frustrating as it is satisfying. Matching babies with parents runs the same range of emotions.

There's no doubt that some of my kids have lifelong challenges they probably wouldn't have if they were my biological children. Two of them spent their prenatal months in a stew of drugs and alcohol that left lifelong residual effects. Learning disabilities, impulse control and anger management are too often the results of an unhealthy prenatal environment. I went into those adoptions with my eyes open, but it's only after you live with the day-to-day demands of a special-needs child that you know what it's like. Because everyone has their own strengths as well as their challenges, mothering special-needs children can be just as gratifying as raising a child with no physical or emotional handicaps.

In our household, everyone has their own life story. Every question that the kids ask is answered honestly. There's nothing to hide. When they were younger, the kids would beg to hear their individual stories, especially on long car rides. Noah's story begins, "It was a dark and stormy night as Noah's brother, sister and mother made their way through a fierce snowstorm to bring him home with them." When Aaron was small, a friend asked him about his dad and he said he was artificially inseminated. The kid went home and told his mother that Aaron had been born in a space program laboratory!

Zachary is the only one who knows his birth family. He's visited them on several occasions. The other kids don't, though that could change when they get older. Noah's birth mother has signed an agreement by which he can look her up when he turns eighteen. I send her occasional pictures through the adoption lawyer.

Samantha's birth mother preferred a closed adoption, though I do have information that can help locate her one day if she wants to. We'd do it through an attorney, so as not to disrupt the birth mother's life. As is often the case in Chinese adoptions, we only know the province were Leah was found, but little else, because of the way the system works there.

I consider the adoption process as a triangle with three connected points—the birth family, the adoptive family and the adopted child. Each has a connection to the other. Some adopted children are afraid to show curiosity about their biological family because they don't want to hurt their adoptive family's feelings. And some adoptive parents feel insecure that if their child seeks out a birth mother that new relationship might diminish their bond. No one questions whether a mother can love two children. Why can't an adoptee love two moms?

When the six of us are out at the mall, I'm often asked questions like, "Which ones are yours?" or "Which ones are real?" Instead of getting mad, I just laugh at their ignorance. When they were little, I'd have my black and white babies, Noah and Zachary, in a double stroller and people would stop me and ask if they were twins. I'd just tell the truth, "No, they're five months apart." Truth is even more strangely wonderful than fiction.

PART SEVEN:

MULTICULTURAL
AND MIXED RACE
ADOPTION

# MICHAEL AND LISA WITH MULI, TEY, IAN AND RACHAEL

● ● ● ● ● ● ● ● ● ● ● ● ● ● ● ● ●

**Lisa**: We met at Stanford when we were both in law school. We never even discussed having children before we got married. Fourteen years ago, we had our only biological child, Rachael. A few years later we both wanted another child. I had always wanted to adopt…

**Michael**: …which was the first I'd heard about it.

**Lisa**: There are so many children in the world who desperately need families and I never had that much invested in carrying on my own genes.

**Michael**: I think Lisa's philosophy behind adoption is a lot like her animal rights activism. There are so many pets and children that need nurturing homes, there's no need to breed more.

**Lisa**: Some people get upset if you use the term adopt with an animal, because it's disrespectful to the human parental commitment. But it doesn't bother me because I also take the responsibility for my animals as a lifelong commitment. Rachael was four when we brought six year old Muli into our lives. The process took a year. It's unusual that our first child is not our oldest child, but we wanted a sister for Rachael, someone close to her in age. The adoption agency sent us photographs of children who were available. My mother and sister fell in love with Muli at the first sight of her picture. But because Muli was such a beautiful child, I wasn't sure if we should adopt her. I was always the tenderhearted kid who picked the runt out of the litter. I knew lots of people would want to adopt Muli, so at first I was more attracted to the crying, sickly babies. I'm glad my family's enthusiasm persevered because I couldn't ask for a more wonderful oldest daughter. And she's been a great sister to Rachael.

**Rachael**: I can remember some things from back then—like looking at pictures of Muli before she came here, and my dad and me meeting them at the airport when my mom brought her back from Ethiopia. We had a little stuffed animal for her—a kitty—that she still has today. She didn't speak much English but she learned it so fast.

I'll almost certainly adopt kids one day.
I'm definitely my mother's daughter when it comes to thinking about all the
little children out there who so badly need a family. —Rachael, age 14

**Muli**: I hardly remember anything about Ethiopia, but I remember trying to stay awake on the flight over to my new home. Mom had brought me this album with pictures of my new Dad, my sister Ray—even the dog.

**Rachael**: I was so excited to have a sister. I remember showing Muli her new room the day she arrived. Even though we had separate bedrooms, I stayed with her the first night. She's always definitely been my older sister, even though I was the first child in the family. She's always reminding me to respect my elders. Sometimes she'll joke and says, "We should adopt someone older than me, so I don't have all the responsibility!"

**Lisa**: A few years after Muli's arrival I started feeling like my family wasn't complete. It needed a brother, a son. The process with the orphanage in Jamaica was painfully slow, so my mother and I decided to take matters into our own hands and go down there.

**Michael**: Lisa's mom was great. She threatened to have a heart attack if the Embassy sent Ian back to the orphanage. It was a bureaucratic maze of confusion. We never would have gotten our son if my mother-in-law hadn't been there to intimidate them!

**Lisa**: Ian was a three and a half by then, after a year of us trying to adopt him. Everyone was relieved to get him home where we knew he belonged.

Michael: The girls were so enthusiastic about Ian's arrival, but they felt a bit deprived of attention when he was first settling in. Everyone was excited about Tey's adoption a few years later, except maybe Ian, who had wanted a six year old brother to play ball with.

**Lisa**: Tey's was a long adoption process too. We were actually going to adopt a little Cambodian boy, but the government started restricting American adoptions.

**Michael**: The Cambodian minister said something like, "I'd rather the children die than go to America." He was still bitter from the Viet Nam war era.

**Lisa**: It's hard for people in third world countries, with such extreme poverty, to understand why American families would be willing to adopt and have large families. So there are all kinds of rumors about Americans buying children for body parts.

**Michael**: Poor countries may consider that too many adoptions from the United States is a form of cultural hegemony. And sometimes it's the American Embassies overseas who shut things down because of allegations of kidnapping of babies to sell for profit. The more destitute the country, the more vulnerable it is to adoption abuse.

**Lisa**: It's frustrating because there are so many orphaned children and potential parents waiting with empty arms. But corruption and politics get in the way. I kept networking the agencies and discovered Tey in an orphanage in Azerbaijan, on the Caspian Sea. Michael and I had to travel there twice in order to adopt her. It's emotionally wrenching because we'd already fallen in

love with her through her pictures before we even met her the first time. Then you have to turn around and leave her in the orphanage before coming back for a second time. It was especially hard to leave her then because she was so malnourished. She weighed twelve and a half pounds at one year and even less when we returned to bring her home.

**Michael**: She couldn't even sit up, much less crawl. Every child at the orphanage was developmentally delayed because the place was so overcrowded and under staffed.

**Lisa**: They do the best they can but they're completely overwhelmed. It breaks your heart to see all these babies crying in their cribs. The staff has no time to comfort them because it's all they can do to keep them fed and clean. It's hard to just bring one baby back, when there are so many little ones in desperate need for love.

**Michael**: Maybe we'll adopt an older child when Tey is home alone, after her brother and sisters go off to college. Older children have a harder time being placed in families, and, after being raised alongside so many siblings, Tey probably won't want to be an only child.

**Rachael**: I'll almost certainly adopt kids one day. I'm definitely my mother's daughter when it comes to thinking about all the little children out there who so badly need a family.

# DUANE AND DEBRA WITH LYDIA

•••••••••••••••••

**Debra**: Duane and I lived together for a long time before we got married seven years ago. We knew we wanted to be parents but we didn't get married until I was almost forty. After three years we started thinking about adoption as a good option to be a mom and a dad. My brother had adopted a child from Guatemala, so he paved the way for us. My job as a special education teacher was good preparation to fill out all the paperwork involved in the South American adoption process. We had to get a recommendation from a minister and be fingerprinted by the FBI. It was a long, arduous process. The hardest part was knowing Lydia was born and having to wait nine months to bring her home. They had sent us a picture of her at one week old and it was love at first sight. We knew she was meant to be our daughter.

**Duane**: It also made us feel good that Lydia's birth mother chose us to be her baby's parents. Call it destiny, fate—whatever you want—but being Lydia's father feels like a perfect fit for me.

**Debra**: I have a belief that we come to this earth to experience whatever lessons we need to learn. I think in a strange way, we all pick our parents. I have a lot of respect for both nature and nurture. Our parenting style will have a big influence on Lydia, for sure. But you can't discount DNA. Lydia brings her genetic legacy into our household and that's all part of who she is—who she needs to be in this lifetime.

**Duane**: The adoption process in Guatemala got bogged down after Lydia was born. Debra and I became so frustrated that we went down there against our agency's wishes. It finally got to the point where we just couldn't be passive anymore. We had to do something. It took us three weeks in Guatemala to get her papers in order and bring her back to the States.

**Debra**: It was so frustrating to be getting photos each month of Lydia and see her slowly losing her vibrancy as she spent time in the orphanage. We couldn't just sit here and do nothing. When we finally got down there, she was nine months old. I'll never forget the moment we were led back into this dark room filled with children.

One thing I wasn't prepared for, being an older mom with a child of a different ethnic background, is how many looks we got in public—people trying to figure us out. At first when people would ask where Lydia was from, I'd feel threatened. I worried they'd think our bond was weaker than if I was her biological mom. The hardest remark is when people ask, "Where's her mom?" I take a deep breath and say, "I'm her mom. Her birth mom lives in Guatemala." —Debra

**Duane**: There were cribs lined up side-by-side and children everywhere, from newborn to ten years old. The staff was making a heroic effort but it was an overwhelming situation. Lydia was definitely shutting down emotionally from all the external stimulation and lack of affection. As soon as we began making daily visits, she started coming out of her shell, smiling and being more responsive.

**Debra**: It was like, "Take one baby, add water!" She just blossomed. We went to the orphanage every day and helped out while we were waiting to bring her home. In their system they wouldn't let the babies be held very much because they'd come to expect it. So we'd cuddle with them for a short while, then put them back in their cribs. The staff were glad to have us around, so long as we didn't make the kids too needy and demanding.

**Duane**: I feel like raising a child from Guatemala is a big responsibility, not only in our obligation to Lydia, but to her family and the caretakers who placed so much hope and trust in us. Everyone there seemed to want her to experience all the opportunities that the United States had to offer. For some people, it seemed as if our adopting Lydia awakened their own dreams, even while knowing that not everyone who wants it can achieve it.

**Debra**: It's like we've become global parents. When we hear of children starving somewhere in the world, we feel it more deeply. It matters much more to us after our time in Guatemala. We know firsthand that suffering is very real and not just a concept.

**Duane**: We met other Americans who were waiting to bring their adopted children home. Some had been there for almost a year. I know it sounds crazy, but believe me, it's worth it. Being parents has been so wonderful for us. We knew we wanted children, even though we had no idea what that really meant until we actually become parents.

**Debra**: One thing I wasn't prepared for, being an older mom with a child of a different ethnic background, is how many looks we got in public—people trying to figure us out. Sometimes they ask if Lydia is Native American. It doesn't bother me as much anymore. At first when people would ask where Lydia was from, I'd feel threatened. I worried they'd think our bond was weaker than if I was her biological mom. The hardest remark is when people ask, "Where's her mom?" I take a deep breath and say, "I'm her mom. Her birth mom lives in Guatemala." Lydia is at the age now where she's listening and interpreting everything. I don't like people questioning my motherhood in front of her.

**Duane**: It's no secret that she's adopted, but children should be reinforced with the similarities within their family, rather than their differences.

**Debra**: Since we've adopted Lydia, I've been amazed to learn how many of the people we know were also adopted. What's especially interesting is how, for some, it's no big deal, but for others it's always an issue. The complexity of human nature is such that there are no guarantees of success for anyone, whether they are adopted or not.

# DENNIS AND SUSAN
# WITH AJA AND JACKIE

•••••••••••••••••

**Susan**: I was divorced when my biological daughter, Rachael, was two years old. I met Dennis when she was sixteen. We married a few years later and have been together for seventeen years. We'd never even discussed having more children. It wasn't something I thought about.

**Dennis**: Me, either. Although I'd never had children, I loved Rachael like my own and neither of us could imagine having more than one child.

**Susan**: Rachael was so perfect, that I couldn't imagine loving another child as much as I did her, so I would never want to do that to another child. Then I read something that ignited a spark in me. I'll never forget. There was a picture on the front page of the *NY Times* Metro Section of a group of little Chinese girls dancing a ribbon dance. The article gave information about an agency that was facilitating the adoption of these abandoned girls. I'd spent the last year thinking about what I was going to do with the rest of my life. Once my only child became an adult, I didn't want to spend the rest of my life just going to work and the movies. I needed to be involved in something that had a deeper connection.

**Dennis**: This was on a Sunday. Susan says, "This sounds like a good idea," to adopt a baby from China. She said she wanted to go to the Wednesday meeting. For me, this is coming out of nowhere. We'd never discussed a family bigger than the three of us. My first reaction was, "Are you crazy!" Then I looked at the article. By the time the meeting rolled around, I was as into it as she was. There was a woman there with a little baby with spiky black hair, and she just looked so cute. I got enthusiastic instead of just curious…

**Susan**: …and I started getting cold feet, thinking I was too old for the task. But the adoption agency had no problem with our ages, because in the Chinese culture the grandparents raise the children. They value the wisdom and experience of age.

**Dennis**: My concern wasn't how to do the paper work, but what you did with the baby after you had her. I was reading all these books, but after a while I realized I could just do what ninety nine percent of the rest of the world does—wait until the baby arrives and just do it. And you know what? It wasn't that difficult.'

**Susan**: At the time, Rachael was twenty five and didn't like the idea. After all, she was used to being an only child. It wasn't until we got Aja home that she was convinced that our plan was an inspiration. Rachael found a baby picture of herself and said, "Don't you think we kind of look alike?" At first I thought she was being humorous. When I realized she was sincere, I knew that she was bonding with this baby girl as much as we were. A few years later, when we decided to adopt a little sister for Aja, both of my daughters were excited about a new sister. When Aja was six, we took her back to her province in China. She asked if the director or the caregiver there knew her birth parents. They went through all her records but there was no information there.

We took her there again when we got Jackie. Now she tells people that she's from China but her parents are from New York. We requested that our second adoption be from the same province as Aja, so we could take both girls back to their birthplace from time to time. They both come from Luoyang in Henan, which is the oldest and poorest province in China. It's the seat of Buddhism on the Silk Road. Since Dennis and I admire the Chinese traditions and encourage the girls to explore their heritage in Luoyang, the girls feel good about their backgrounds. In China they say everyone gets the child they're supposed to have. I'm so glad they were chosen for us.

**Dennis**: When we were tucking Aja her into bed one evening, she said, "I wonder what my Chinese mother looks like and if she wonders how I'm doing." Having these two little girls in our lives has really expanded our horizons, and not only about an entirely different culture. It's also their combination of innocence and wisdom which are so extraordinary that it makes me see the world through new eyes.

# ANGELA AND JERRY
# WITH LEXI AND JAY JAY

● ● ● ● ● ● ● ● ● ● ● ● ● ● ● ● ●

**Jerry**: We had talked about the possibility of adoption before we even tried to conceive a child…

**Angela**: …because I had been married before and had never gotten pregnant. Jerry and I did the whole IVF thing three times. There was no pregnancy on the first and the third rounds. The second time, I miscarried at sixteen weeks. I was heartbroken and depressed but Jerry helped me see that we could still have a family together.

**Jerry**: I was comfortable with adoption. One of my best friends growing up was adopted. He had a wonderful family and a happy childhood. Adoption seemed like a good thing.

**Angela**: We worked with an adoption agency where the birth mothers get to choose the adoptive parents. Four months after we did the paperwork, we were contacted by Lexi's mother in Texas to come meet with her. She was only fifteen and in foster care with her seven month old daughter, Lexi. So we got to meet our baby, her birth mother and the foster mother. The birth mother wanted an open adoption and we agreed to keep in touch through the years. We also got an 800 number and gave it to her so she could call anytime. When we got home and told the adoption agency that we wanted to adopt the baby girl in Texas, they asked if we'd like to have a son as well. A baby boy had been born that day and was available immediately. We drove to the hospital where Jay Jay was and took him home with us. His birth mother was twenty one years old, already had three children at home, and had given another one up for adoption. She didn't want to stay in contact with us but she did ask us to send pictures from time to time.

**Jerry**: When we went back to Texas to get Lexi, it was emotionally wrenching. Even though her birth mother knew she couldn't raise her—she was just a child herself—the birth mother's *foster* mother had gotten so attached that *she* wanted to keep the baby. But Lexi's mother was adamant. She wanted her child to have both a father and a mother, which was something neither she nor the foster

> **Living in a mixed family makes you much more aware of assumptions about race. It's been a healing experience for my family. Now that my parents have fallen in love with their black grandchildren, they're able to accept a black son-in-law. —Jerry**

mother could offer. There were many tears and prayers when they handed her over and I think Lexi was depressed for a month or two after she came home with us. She'd obviously gotten attached to them.

**Angela**: When we first got her home, all she cared about was her bottle. It took time for her to get attached to us. Now she loves us as much as any child loves her parents. Coincidentally, Jerry's sister had been a relationship with a black man for ten years. It caused all kinds of family tension and her parents had threatened to disown her if she married him. Now, they're getting married. We think that our multiracial family helped Jerry's parents overcome their prejudice. They certainly weren't pleased when we adopted outside of our race but we knew that these children needed a loving home and we were longing for a family. Jerry's father couldn't help but love Lexi and Jay Jay once they were in our family. And now, at long last, he's reaching out to his daughter's fiancé.

**Jerry**: Some of my friends at work say they admire my willingness to adopt black children, but they could never do it themselves. For me, there was nothing admirable about it. I feel lucky to be a father to these two wonderful kids.

**Angela**: Because we live in a university town, there are other mixed race families and quite a bit of diversity but when we go to rural areas, our family attracts stares. I know that when the kids become teenagers we'll face more race issues, but you can't make decisions based on fear of the unknown.

**Jerry**: I read a book called *Why Are All the Black Children Sitting Together in the Cafeteria?* It gives insight into the prejudices ingrained in all of us. Living in a mixed family makes you more aware of assumptions about race. It's been a healing experience for my family. Now that my parents have fallen in love with their black grandchildren, they're able to accept a black son-in-law.

**Angela**: My parents didn't like the idea of us adopting outside of our race either. But once it became clear that Lexi and Jay Jay were going to be their grandchildren, they accepted them wholeheartedly. It was Jerry's mother who first confronted his father's prejudice. She put her foot down and said she wasn't going to let anything get in the way of her relationship with her son—that his family would always be welcome in their home. Now his dad loves our kids so much, he'd be the first one to come to their defense.

PART EIGHT:

SPECIAL NEEDS

# MIKE AND SUSAN WITH CAMILLE

•••••••••••••••

**Susan**: When our oldest daughter was thirteen and our son was ten, Mike met Camille in the Hilltop Home for severely retarded children. He was there as a pediatrician, not a potential parent. I was recovering from breast cancer and we weren't looking to take on another child. But the first time Mike walked into that institution and saw this beautiful little brown eyed, blond haired girl in a wheel chair, he was immediately drawn to her. He felt from the moment he met her that she didn't belong there. He started bringing her home on weekends, so he could assess her abilities. Our initial impulse was to be Camille's advocate. We thought if we could figure out a way for her to communicate, despite the damage to her brain and body, it would help her get adopted. And, as they say, "the rest is history." In no time it was obvious that she loved being part of our family. She'd wave her arms when Mike would walk through the door and smile whenever she saw us. Even though she can't speak, her face is so responsive. It was definitely a family project. Our daughter was especially keen on trying to help Camille come out of her shell. It was more of an adjustment for our son, who had to give up his position as the youngest child. What really began to bother all of us was that she belonged to the State. She'd start to cry as soon as we headed out of our driveway on Sunday to bring her back to Hilltop Home. We realized we felt the same about her. So we got our foster care license so we could have her live with us full time.

**Mike**: I just had love at first sight when I saw her. That's not rational, but it doesn't make it less real. We feel like Camille found us as much as we found her.

**Susan**: When she first came into our lives I was at the point where I finally had the time to focus on my artwork. I was afraid that having a young child in the house, especially a special needs child, would drain away my creative energy. In hindsight, it had quite the opposite effect. There was such a learning curve for all of us that it was stimulating and exciting. The progress we made together felt so good, it became inspirational.

Once she began living with us full time, we enrolled her in special classes for kids with cerebral palsy. Later she entered the public school system. When my father retired, he used his time to create language wheels and interactive toys for her.

> **Raising a child like Camille teaches you lessons about patience and determination that you'd never figure out on your own. The more you slow down and pay attention, instead of talking and telling, the better you are at truly communicating.** —Mike

He created a mouth switch so she could bite down when the wheel got to the word she wanted. This was before people had personal computers in their homes. Even though she doesn't have the use of her hands or feet, and her torso is floppy, she has enough motor control to use a head switch to operate a keyboard and now she uses a computer to communicate.

Today she lives with her boyfriend. They met when he was a counselor at Camp Easter Seals. He's completely devoted to her. Like us, he fell for her in a big way. When you're around them any length of time, you can tell they're genuinely crazy about each other. They're both thirty now and have been together seven years. They used to live with us, but now they have their own townhouse. He works for IBM and has been instrumental in helping Camille with computer communication. Every morning when he leaves for work, an aide comes and stays with Camille until 2:00 PM. Then we bring her here, where she usually listens to books on tape, which she loves. Her boyfriend joins us for dinner, and afterwards we drive her back to their place in our van, which can transport her wheel chair.

**Mike**: At three she was very much like she is today, smiling and catching you with her watchful eyes. I knew she had more potential than she'd ever discover in a group home, so I enlisted the rest of the family on a mission to help her. Once they met her, it wasn't hard to get their support. She's taught us as much as we've taught her in

the past twenty seven years together. For example, when she'd call out in the night, I needed a way to figure out how to answer her needs as smoothly as possible so everyone could get back to sleep. Together we learned how to communicate in the dark. I'd put my hand by her cheek and ask her questions. To answer "yes," she'd turn her head and touch my hand with her cheek. We taught each other as we went along. The computer has enabled Camille to be able to express her feelings as well as her needs. The other day she typed, "Dad, I'm not a teenager anymore!" She even manages her own finances on-line. Daily, weekly, monthly, through the years, raising a child like Camille teaches you lessons about patience and determination that you'd never figure out on your own. I have no doubt that I was able to be a better doctor because of the values Camille taught me. It made me even more aware of how important it is to take my time and pay attention to my patients. The more you slow down and pay attention, instead of always talking and telling, the better you are at truly communicating. She taught me to listen with my eyes and my touch as well as with my ears.

**Susan**: Having her join our household juiced up my creative energy and made me more prolific.

**Mike**: Her handicaps taught us to take risks…

**Susan**: …and also to quickly get over caring about what other people think, which in itself is liberating.

**Mike**: When you go through medical training, everything is planned ahead years in advance. One step leads to another without much variation. But when you encounter an opportunity like Camille, it's transformative. We've taken risks in our lives that we wouldn't have had the confidence to do if we hadn't gone through what we did raising Camille.

# NYM AND ALLEGRA WITH NOAH, BOOKER AND MUSCLE

••••••••••••••••

**Allegra**: When my biological daughter Ana was six years old, I adopted my first son, Robert. I was a single mom then, working for social services in group homes serving hard-to-place children who are in foster care. Robert's foster father of four years had developed a drinking problem and Robert was removed and placed into a group home at the age of seven. He was basically catatonic with grief. It touched my heart, and I knew I had to take him. He needed constant attention. Every night he woke up with night terrors and his days were filled with defiant, often violent behavior. At twelve he had a psychotic breakdown followed by delinquent teenage years and an eventual brush with death—a bullet lodged under his heart. Now, at the age of twenty seven, he's an A student in college with the sweetest girlfriend, a great job and an affirming attitude.

**Nym**: He signs his letters to us "The Good One." He's a really great guy.

**Allegra**: When I got the call from social services telling me about Noah, I couldn't turn away. He was in a home for medically fragile infants and in dire need of parents. My specialty is body mechanics and neurological function, so I knew I could give him the needed care. Like Robert, he came with his own set of problems but the rewards have been so worthwhile. Adopting children, especially those with special needs, challenges your parenting skills and demands the best from you. It's a humbling experience, requiring a lot of soul-searching to do what's right for each child's unique set of problems.

When we adopted Booker, he had such terrible upper respiratory damage that every breath was a frightening struggle. The phenobarbital used to get him through methadone withdrawal had left scar tissue in his respiratory tract. And our son Muscle was born premature. He had seizures and needed physical therapy to help overcome his neurological problems.

Noah, Booker and Muscle all have the same mother, who has four other children placed with another family. She's half German, half Cherokee and a lifelong drug addict. She's had many chances to rehabilitate and keep her children, but she simply can't. I had the chance to meet her because she was in jail when Booker was born. She didn't know who I was at first, but I recognized her right away because Noah looks so much like her. When we made eye contact through the glass partition, we both started crying. She knew I was there to see her, but she had no idea who I was. There was just this immediate emotional connection. Then I told her, "I'm mothering three of your children, and showed her their pictures.

**Nym**: Unfortunately, we only have limited knowledge about her. We don't even know where she is now. Because of the boys' medical records, we know what drugs she was on while pregnant, but that's about it.

**Allegra**: People expect me to be angry with her about her behavior but I'm not. I feel a bond, a sense of protectiveness. I've seen her files. She had a horribly abusive childhood. She's been diagnosed bipolar and, for her, drug abuse started out as a way of self-medicating. Some people are dealt bad cards and their life circumstances make it impossible for them to rise. I believe that every time she had a child it was her way of saying "yes" to life. After meeting her in prison and reading her file, I know she's a sweet, simple person who's been badly damaged. Her addictions simply overcame her. Who am I to judge?

**Nym** When I married Allegra, she already had Ana—who by this time was grown with a child of her own—and Robert and Noah. I immediately went from being an impatient bachelor artist to being a husband, father and grandfather. Now I believe that raising children, especially those who have special needs and really need a family, is even more important than art. You don't need to paint the Mona Lisa to be doing something truly important. It's fun to be a dad but it's also hard work. And humbling, too. The boys are so physically active, they really need a dad to kick a ball around with. And I'm the one Muscle wants when he wakes up in the night. I've never had biological children, but I can't imagine loving kids more than the ones who call me Dad.

Before I met Allegra, I was fearful of being a parent, adoptive or otherwise. Once these kids were in my life because of my love for Allegra, I had to rise to the occasion. It's one of the best things that ever happened to me. I had a terrible head injury myself the year before we met. That's made me more sympathetic towards our boys because I know that neurological damage can have a tremendous influence on behavior.

**Allegra**: People are basically good when they're brought to the test. But in our society we have so many *things* that we've become careless. Outer riches displace inner riches—too much external stuff stifles creativity and all of our screaming machines thwart imagination. That's why I love the Waldorf education system. It nurtures that special individuality in all of us.

**Nym**: Look at what television offers—celebrity worship, brand worship, a bunch of empty junk with nothing of substance. As an artist, I don't make a lot of money– which is how we measure success in our society—but I get tremendous satisfaction from my work. Having a family, I can't paint every day like I did when I was single, but when I do, I enjoy it more. And my paintings are more playful and less monstrous since I've become a parent.

**Allegra**: One difference between us and many other adoptive parents is that the children

just came to us. Even with Robert, I wasn't looking to adopt. But once I saw him languishing in that group home, I knew I couldn't leave him there. Social services called us about Noah, Booker, and Muscle and, with each phone call, I knew it was meant to be. It's my spiritual belief that you meet them when you can handle them. And if it's meant to be, I'm wide open to more children.

**Nym**: When you adopt a child, especially a special needs child, it takes faith that you can do the right things for them. We've had tremendous pressure from doctors

to medicate them with behavior modifying drugs, but we believe they're better served with positive behavior modifying techniques.

**Allegra**: I would never medicate the child of a drug addict with mood altering drugs. A diagnosis and prescription may rearrange the symptoms but it won't get at the problem. There are physical therapies and parenting techniques that amend the behavior without clouding brain function. It takes time and consciousness, but it's worth it.

**Nym**: For example, if I want to ask Muscle a question, I'll place my hand on him before I speak. It helps him concentrate on a response.

**Allegra**: Nurturing your children, you become more self-aware. Or at least you should, if you give it the attention it deserves. Nym and I are always talking about new approaches to help our kids develop. That introspection teaches you about who you are and who you want to be. When people call us saintly for taking on these kids, I tell them that they're as good for us as we are for them.

# DIANE WITH COREY, GERALDINE AND GERALD

**Diane:** I'd wanted to be a mom for as long as I can remember, but in my thirties there was still no Mr. Right. I realized I was going to have to be creative if I was going to raise children. The most unique thing about my four adopted children is they're all children of HIV positive mothers. At the time my kids were born, it took up to a year to get test results to find out whether they were infected. Now there are much more sensitive tests that can tell within a few days whether the infant is HIV positive or negative. Three of the four babies I adopted eventually tested negative for the virus.

At that time in Newark, the foster care system was overwhelmed with HIV positive infants. Many of these infants were boarded in hospitals because foster and adoptive parents were afraid. As a medical social worker specializing in HIV case work, I could separate fact from fiction and wasn't afraid to take the risk. I got a call in June about the twins, who had been born months before but had never left the hospital because there wasn't any place for them to go. I took Gerald and Geraldine as a foster mother because at that point their mother wasn't ready to relinquish them for adoption. The Division of Youth and Family Services provided someone to help take care of the twins, because with no husband I had to continue to earn an income. Medicaid helped cover their medical expenses, so I was able to get them the medical care they needed. Fortunately this wasn't much, as they both tested negative for the virus by their first birthday. I also had a lot of family and community support. I might be a single mom, but I never felt alone.

The hardest time was ten months after they'd come to live with me. The twins' birth mother showed up and took them back to live with her. I cried for twenty four hours, none stop, like my heart had been taken away. I was already visiting Corey in a HIV group home when he was seven months old. He was available for adoption and I was planning on bringing him home about two weeks after Geraldine and Gerald left. During that time I got a phone call about a baby girl who'd been rescued from a crack house. I'd cared for twins before, so I said, "Might as well have two as one." When I picked her up from Family Services, little Keya was so sick and dirty. There was no doubt in my mind that I could do some good. Corey arrived soon after.

I stayed in touch with Geraldine and Gerald's social worker and still visited them from time to time. Their mother was struggling with substance abuse and didn't have much in the way of support systems. When it became clear that twins would be placed back in foster care, I had no doubt they belonged with me, despite now having two other infants to care for. Soon, I had four children, ages one and under. I had four high chairs and cribs and over two hundred dollars a month in diaper bills! The four kids always got along, so that was a great help. I'd put the two smallest in a front and back carrier and the two larger ones in a double stroller. I must have looked like a circus act!

Several years later, Keya started showing symptoms of HIV. She lost her appetite and dropped weight. Back then, there weren't the medications like there are now to help the immune system. The three other kids had all tested negative by then, but Keya needed to be hospitalized by the time she was four. The twins' birth mother was our saving grace during that time, because she'd come over and stay with the other three kids. The Make A Wish Foundation sent the whole family to Disney World in February and Keya passed away in March. She had told me several months before that, "Mommy, I'm ready to go see God." She died at home, watching cartoons with the other kids. I was holding her in my arms peacefully when she closed her eyes forever.

Her funeral was a celebration of a little life that wasn't long enough. She would have been five in June.

**Geraldine**: I remember Mom holding her and everyone being so quiet. There was an unusual calm in the room. And I remember Mom giving her a bath after she died, and dressing her in her pretty purple dress. She was limp and still but I didn't get it until the house started filling up with family and friends.

**Diane**: The kids wanted to celebrate Keya's birthday a few months after she died. We got a cake and purple balloons. Just like at her funeral, we let the balloons float up into the sky.

**Geraldine**: I believe that somehow she received those balloons.

**Diane**: Soon after, the twins' birth mother became very ill with HIV. I would take them to the hospital to see her. They called her "Gloria" and me "Mom," but I wanted to make sure that they knew their biological mom before she died. It meant a lot for Gloria to see them before she passed away. When the kids get their school pictures every year, I always get an extra set for Gloria's sister and parents, who, like Gloria, don't speak English.

**Gerald**: Geraldine and I are studying Spanish in school, but it's hard to learn to speak a language in a classroom. I may look Puerto Rican, but I don't feel it.

**Diane**: An even bigger surprise for people who don't know our family is when Corey is introduced as Geraldine's brother.

**Corey**: Both Geraldine and Gerald knew their birth mom, but I never did. She's probably died from AIDS by now, but I don't think about it much. I know how good I have it here.

**Diane**: When Corey was little and Gloria would come to visit the twins, he'd ask "Where's *my* other mom?" He'd cry, which would make me cry too, because I didn't have an answer. Keya's mom visited once, then I didn't hear news of her again until I saw her obituary.

**Geraldine**: Even though Keya was even darker skinned than Corey, I never noticed the difference. We both played with white Barbie dolls. It wasn't until we started school and other kids would ask questions that I thought about it. We just felt like brothers and sisters and didn't give our skin color much thought.

**Diane**: We were so fortunate to have Keya with us. We have a strong faith that's carried us though the hard times and blessed us with much happiness.

**Corey**: Even though I'm the only black person in our church, I never even notice. No one treats me any different than the rest. But it's sometimes uncomfortable to hang out with the black kids at school, because I wasn't raised in that culture.

**Geraldine**: Like Gerald and me. We don't have much involvement in Latino culture.

**Diane**: The three of them have always been so close growing up, have always been there for each other. They all have friends, but are each other's best friends. It'll be mighty quiet around here when the three of them go off to college. I've enjoyed each stage of their growing up so much, especially these teenage years. And I'm looking forward to being a grandma. But not too soon!

PART NINE:

LGBT ADOPTION

# JEFFREY AND STEVEN
# WITH THEIR SON, LUCAS

●●●●●●●●●●●●●●●●

**Steven**: We've been together for eighteen years. As a young man, I assumed I'd never be a father because of my sexual orientation. But after Jeffrey and I spent three weeks in Australia with a friend and her adorable nine month old baby, we came back knowing that parenthood is something we wanted to share and experience. Some of our gay friends couldn't understand our desire to be parents, but we wanted a life that was larger than just thinking about ourselves. I remember saying to a group of friends that I needed to leave and go pick up our baby. Someone asked, "What breed?" and I shocked them when I said, "Human!"

**Jeffrey**: Eight or ten years ago, a gay couple adopting an infant was far from the norm. In fact, there was very little discussion on the subject in the press until several years ago, well after we had adopted Lucas. In hindsight, I realize we were pioneers—thanks in no small part to the incredible lawyers that we worked with. We made a little book about our backgrounds and situation and gave it to the adoption agency who, in turn, showed it to prospective birth mothers. We had a match soon afterwards, and a few months later we were in the delivery room. In fact, Steven cut the cord. The nurses were a little perplexed having two dads at the delivery, but we persevered!

**Steven**: Unlike a straight couple, there are no traditional parenting roles with two Dads. Because I was working at home when Lucas was born, I did, in the beginning, spend more time with him, even though we had full time help. One advantage to being male is that when the pediatrician says you can stop nighttime feedings, you're okay with letting the baby wake up and cry himself back to sleep. The doctor said it would help him learn to sleep through the night. And, in fact, after just a few days, Lucas *was* sleeping through the night instead of crying. Our female friends often complained they were so tired because their child was waking them up constantly in the night. Jeffery and I couldn't understand why they didn't just ignore it.

> Some of our gay friends couldn't understand our desire to be parents. I wanted to move on to a life that was larger than just thinking about Jeffrey and myself. I remember saying to a group of friends that I needed to leave to go pick up our baby. Someone asked, "What breed?" and I shocked them when I said, "Human!"  —Steven

**Jeffrey**: I think there's much less hysteria on the part of men when it comes to a fussy baby. We can be more nonchalant. Of course, you certainly want to fulfill your child's needs, but the crying itself doesn't emotionally rip us apart like it did our friends who were mothers instead of fathers.

**Steven**: Women I'd encounter while out with Lucas would have one of two reactions; either, "Oh that's so wonderful, you're giving Mom a day off," or "Where the hell is Mom?" And women would continually come up and ask Lucas, "Where is your mother?" They couldn't believe I was willing or capable of taking care of a young baby. It wasn't because of our sexual orientation that we were suspect as parents, but because we were men! Surely we'd drop him, or forget to change or feed him! Fortunately those attitudes passed by the time Lucas was in kindergarten.

**Lucas**: Sometimes people ask me if I'm adopted and I say "Yes." They usually say "That's cool," or "Me, too!"

**Jeffrey**: Because divorce is so common and younger children usually stay with their mothers, it's fun when his friends are over. They get to be with two dads instead of none.

**Lucas**: I have a friend, Emma, who has two moms!

**Steven**: When I called my parents in England to tell them they were going to be grandparents, they were surprised, to put it mildly. In fact, they were not at all encouraging. They said it was wrong and we shouldn't do it. But I've always kept my own counsel on important issues. Once Lucas was a child instead of a concept, their curiosity got the better of them. And they were so brimming over with good advice that they had to call. Now Lucas goes to England every summer and stays with his grandparents. Having a child has made me much closer to my parents. It gives everyone a whole new point of view. When we're visiting England, I find myself wanting to take Lucas to revisit all the places I went to as a child.

**Jeffrey**: Yes, having a child brings your own childhood into focus. Sometimes you hear your parents' words coming right out of your mouth!

# SUSAN AND CAROL WITH EMMA, JOYA, RAINA AND WILLY

••••••••••••••••

**Susan**: Carol and I met twenty five years ago while I was a resident and she was a medical student. It's hard to believe so much time has gone by. Babies I helped deliver are now in their twenties.

**Carol**: I moved into Susan's house as a roommate to help with the mortgage and we became more than friends. Our neighbor, who was also a lesbian, had a baby by artificial insemination and we were involved in that child's life from the beginning. So parenthood was always something that was a possibility for us too. When I was a little girl, my sister and I would pretend that we had all these adopted children. My childhood imagination was always about motherhood rather than marriage. Susan and I ended up commuting back and forth to see each for over seven years while I was in residency and at the National Health Service Corps. Then we were able to able to settle down and entertain the possibility of children.

**Susan**: Because we were finally going to live together for the first time in seven years, and both of us would have new jobs and possibly a new house, we did some counseling together, just to be prepared. It was through that process that I became aware that I needed to be generative within the relationship—I needed to bring a child into the family. It would be easy for Carol to claim motherhood if she birthed a child through artificial insemination. I wanted to be a mother in the family too, not just a mom's partner.

In the spring of 1989, I was on the postpartum floor in the hospital and a social worker was there with photos of her daughter, who she was waiting to adopt from India. She said, "Susan, you can do this, too." She really captured my attention. We talked about her adoption process and I called the agency the next day.

**Carol**: We had planned to adopt first, before I got pregnant, because Susan is eleven years older than me. We had all the paperwork in place when we got a letter from the agency. It said adoptions from India were on hold while the adoption agencies were being re-credentialed. By that time, we really had our hearts set on having a baby by the next summer, so I decided to go ahead with

> **Having these four kids changed our relationship with the straight community. Other parents realized that we have more in common with them than they thought. We become real, not just an idea that they read about. Everyone came to the realization that we all want the same things for our children, regardless of our sexual orientation. —Carol**

artificial insemination. Two weeks later, I was pregnant! Even though I conceived with a white donor, I imagined I was pregnant with an Indian baby, because that is what we'd been imagining for months. Emma was born at the end of August.

**Susan:** Carol was incredibly generous with the baby, in a way that most new mothers are not. I didn't feel excluded at all. When Emma was five months old, the agency contacted us about a baby girl, Payal, who was available, and we said "Yes!" Two weeks later they called to tell us that Payal had died. That was like a miscarriage for me. I didn't expect to be as grief stuck as I was, knowing about Payal for only two weeks. It was really hard, even though ten days later they had another newborn girl available. Eight weeks later, I went to New Delhi to bring Joya home. I stayed in India for two weeks while the paperwork was completed. Going to India was an incredible, wonderful experience. I met the most amazing people, with whom I'm still in contact. It was so important that I could tell Joya about the women who took care of her, about what her life in the adoption agency was like, and what India was like. Joya was three months and Emma was eight months when Joya and I came home from India.

**Carol:** I would have loved to go with Susan, but with a nursing baby it would have been too hard. I actually breastfed Joya when she first arrived and pumped my breast milk for her bottles. She had lost a lot of weight from being sick, so it felt good to feed her. Now we were

two moms with two daughters. We loved it, absolutely loved it.

**Susan:** Carol's practice was growing; she was doing family practice and also took care of her own obstetric patients. I had a very active Ob/Gyn practice and once a week was required to spend 24 hours on call in the hospital. Our schedules were so chaotic with two young children, so I stopped doing obstetrics. Then Carol sold her private practice to an HMO, which meant she could get paid vacation and maternity leave. As soon as things calmed down, we started thinking about more kids. We had each grown up in families with four kids. That seemed like a nice number to us...

**Carol:** ...and I wanted to get pregnant again. When we told the girls that we were going to adopt another baby, they wanted to know if they were going to get another mom too! It took me longer to get pregnant the next time—by then I was forty years old. I didn't conceive Willy until Susan brought Raina home from India. So Raina and Willy are nineteen months apart but arrived ten months apart in our family. Vermont is one of the few states that allows second parent adoptions by lesbian and gay couples. We were each able to adopt our non-biological children so that all of our kids have two legal parents We created Smithayer as a surname for the kids, by combining the "th" from the end of Smith and the beginning of Thayer.

Having these four kids changed our relationship with the straight community. Other parents realized that we have more in common with them than they thought. We became real, not just an idea that they read about. Everyone came to the realization that we all want the same things for our children, regardless of our sexual orientation.

**Susan:** We don't experience much homophobia in our lives, living in a large community of lesbian and gay families and supportive straight families. But a few years ago we were reminded that not every place is like Burlington, Vermont. Our city has yearly "International Games" with Burlington, Ontario, and it was our turn to host the visiting players. We had two young players staying with us. After the first day, we were told that one of the girls wasn't comfortable in our household. The other kid said she didn't feel well and had to leave too. We had been having a wonderful time together so we couldn't help but suspect their sudden departure was more about who we are rather than anything we did. Emma and Joya were devastated. Thankfully, the whole family had been invited to a birthday party for a child in our school, where we feel warmly accepted and valued by people who know and care for us.

**Carol:** Not that we haven't experienced some weird comments from strangers.

And Mama Susan held Baby Raina and she cried because she was so happy.

And she told Baby Raina "I love you Raina and I'll love you forever. And you have another mommy, Mommy Carol, and two sisters, Emma and Joya who will love you forever too!"

Probably most transcultural families have to deal with them. When Emma and Joya were babies, people would ask us if they were twins. One time someone asked me how far apart in age they were. When I said "Five months," she looked perplexed, then said, "In my day, you had to wait nine months."

Last year we made a trip to India with all the kids. We traveled on a tour with eight other families, all with girls adopted from India. We got to visit places that we never would have seen if we'd traveled on our own. We visited the adoption nursery in the hospital where Joya was born and where both girls had been cared for. We met several of their caregivers and the doctor who delivered Joya and supervised Joya's and Raina's care. Everyone also met the social workers who had managed their adoptions. We still keep in touch with them.

It has been such an unexpected gift to have these children in our lives, to be a transcultural family. It has opened up a whole new culture for us, one that we would not otherwise have had access to, certainly not in in this way. Our family has opened us up to new experiences, new ways to look at the world. We've been so warmly welcomed by the Indian community in our town, and have felt that India has opened her heart to us when we've visited.

PART TEN:

FOSTER HOMES,
ORPHANAGES AND
INSTITUTIONALIZATION

# ANDREW AND LIZ WITH HATTIE, KEENE AND OLEG

●●●●●●●●●●●●●●●

**Liz**: Keene was born two and a half years after Hattie and common sense would have dictated that we had a daughter and a son and were done. But about ten days after Keene was born, I turned to Andrew and said, "I really feel like I've left something at the hospital.'

**Oleg**: They had to go all the way to Russia to find me!

**Liz**: It turns out Oleg and Keene are only ten days apart in age and that day that I felt I'd left something behind at the hospital was August 2nd, Oleg's birthday. Of course, we had no way of knowing that at the time.

**Oleg**: God told my parents how to find me all the way over there.

**Liz**: We were lucky enough to have two healthy children and the means to raise them. We both felt that there are so many kids in the world that need a family that we should offer one a place in our home instead of conceiving another child. Funnily enough, with his green eyes, Oleg looks more like me than my biological children. We knew that there were plenty of couples looking to adopt infants with no medical problems, and so we were willing to take in an older at-risk child. United Methodist Services specializes in adoption of older special needs kids. They make you examine what you can handle and what your expectations are.

**Andrew**: We went in with these idealist notions, but the agency was great at helping us realize our obligations to the two young children we already had. They warned us about taking on a child that might have more special needs than we could fulfill.

**Liz**: If you've ever gone on-line and surfed the web for children available for adoption, it breaks your heart. It's overwhelming to see all the pictures and read the bios. That's where we found Oleg's picture. He looked at least a year younger than he was and we weren't told his real age until a few weeks before were scheduled to arrive at the orphanage in Russia.

**Andrew**: Dealing with the paperwork in Russia seemed never ending. It took weeks to get things sorted out after we arrived. We'd spend the days in the Siberian orphanage. "Dreary" and "bleak" is the only way to describe the

> **Kids who have been deprived of love in an orphanage will often regress to infant-like behavior once they feel secure, because they need to make up for all the nurturing they missed as babies.** —Liz

town. It would have taken even longer to get him, but he had a cleft palate that required surgery so we were able to get him out of there more quickly. His belly was distended over skinny legs bowed with rickets because the cleft palate had made it impossible for him to get enough nutrition.

**Liz**: Back in the states, when he had his mouth surgery the doctors discovered he was partially deaf from scar tissue in his ear canals. He'd had terrible ear infections, but he never let on because they don't have any staff to comfort him. Kids from these kind of institutions will throw themselves on the ground and become totally unresponsive when they're in pain or afraid. They don't cry because it does no good.

**Andrew**: But Oleg would sometimes do more than that. He'd bang his head on the floor, or drag himself over to a wall and bang his head on the wall. It was his way to block out pain and frustration.

**Liz**: It's almost beyond description to see all those children in the orphanage. When we got home, I couldn't get those children out of my mind.

**Oleg**: I had a friend there who had hands like this. (Raising his hands and lowering his middle fingers, leaving only thumbs and pinkies exposed.)

**Liz**: Oleg seemed so afraid of us when we first met him, that I felt he'd gotten this far with another family and had

been rejected. We really had a hard time penetrating his protective surface.

**Andrew**: He was in a room with about fifteen kids between three and five. Every child in that room knew that we were their best chance for a ticket out of there. But Oleg totally clammed up every time we approached. He'd suck his hands and stare into space—wouldn't look at us at all. All the other kids were climbing over us, while Oleg turned away. It took us several days before he would let us touch even him. We were getting more and more attached to all the other children, while the little boy we came to adopt seemed autistic in his behavior.

**Liz**: We began to have serious second thoughts. When I tried to delay the court date, the lawyer started calling me all sorts of terrible names in Russian. He told Andrew he was sorry he had to be married to such a hardheaded woman. I said, "I don't see you adopting a child!" Our court date was delayed through the weekend. On Monday our lawyer didn't show up. But meanwhile, we had taken took Oleg out of the orphanage and Andrew had swooped him up in the air, toward the trees.

**Andrew**: He actually laughed out loud.

**Liz**: The evening before we went to meet with the judge, Oleg looked into a mirror and pointed at Andrew's reflection. "Papa," he said, and then pointed at my reflection and said, "Mama." Then he turned around and looked into my face for the first time. It was just for a moment, but it gave us hope.

**Andrew**: We had learned that his older brother had been adopted and that Oleg had been left behind. We just couldn't bear for him to be rejected again.

**Liz**: Andrew made a moving plea before the court about how Oleg belonged in our family. He said there was no way we could go home without him. We later learned from the nurses at the orphanage that even though Oleg wouldn't look at us when we were there, as soon as we left he'd spend hours looking out the window, waiting for us to return.

**Andrew**: We finally got him to Moscow and had his medical records translated into English. We discovered that the orphanage had been less than honest with us, because neurological damage was listed on his infant assessment. But then we were told that in order to do an out-of-country adoption, it's routine to note neurological damage, because Russia won't allow healthy children to be adopted outside the country. In any event, by then there was no going back on Oleg any more than our other two children. Once we had taken that leap of faith and decided

he was ours, he quickly opened up and bonded with us. By the time we got home, it was like he'd figured out he'd just won the lottery. His first night at supper, he dug into a bowl of soup like it was ice cream and started playing with Hattie and Keene. Now he's all smiles, all Mr. Hugs, and Mr. I Love You.

**Liz**: Not that we haven't had to deal with the residual effects of the orphanage isolation. In some ways, we still do. He'd have awful night terrors…

**Andrew**: …and he cried himself to sleep for the first six months.

**Liz**: Kids who have been deprived of love in an orphanage will often regress to infant-like behavior once they feel secure, because they need to make up for all the nurturing they missed as babies. At first, Oleg was like that. After five years as a part of our family, the surgeries on his palate and ears, and years of speech therapy and special education, he's actually growing into his biological age. Even though both boys are eight years old, Keene has naturally had the role of big brother because Oleg was so delayed when we adopted him. I know that nurturing and loving him has been as good for Hattie and Keene as it has been for Oleg.

# JEFF AND LYNN WITH SETH, LINDSEY AND ILSA

•••••••••••••••••

**Lynn**: When we weren't able to conceive children, I was comfortable with the idea of adoption. My own mother was adopted and had given up a baby for adoption. Once we started going through all that infertility stuff, I realized I'd rather adopt. But, in its own way, adoption was just as hard. It took us five years to adopt Seth. We decided on the name Seth because it means "he who is chosen."

**Jeff**: There was a call on our answering machine to come pick him up at 8:00 AM the next morning. We didn't tell anybody, because two months before we'd been supposed to adopt a child who turned out to be too sick to adopt. That was such a heartbreak, we didn't tell anyone the second time.

**Lynn**: When we went into the Children's Home Society, I thought he was the prettiest thing I'd ever seen in my life. I started crying and told my husband, "All these years I thought we were being punished for something. But now I realize that we're blessed and that we just had to wait for that blessing." What was really wonderful is how we totally surprised everybody when we showed up with our new son.

**Jeff**: Seth was definitely worth the wait. His baseball interferes with the fishing, and football takes time away from hunting, but I don't complain because he's such a great kid!

**Lynn**: When he was about four years old we tried to add to our family, but we couldn't get another infant and I didn't want to get a child older than Seth. Two years later we had another disappointment. We were supposed to go to New Mexico to get a baby daughter but the birth mother changed her mind at the last minute. Another time, social services came out to do a home visit. You could tell immediately the lady didn't like us because of the deer heads on the walls.

**Jeff**: Some kind of anti-hunting thing, I guess.

**Lynn**: The list goes on. We were supposed to get this poor little crack addicted infant, but her drug addict mother decided to keep her. Then there was this mother who had a Hispanic baby that we were supposed to adopt, until it was born looking white, so the agency gave her to a family who could pay more money. After so many heartbreaks, we decided to go overseas to adopt. I felt like I'd lost four babies through domestic adoption and I just couldn't bear to go through that again. Neither of us had any problem adopting a Chinese girl, except for the travel to get her. I'd never crossed an ocean in my life.

**Jeff**: I wouldn't fly in an airplane if you paid me! I'd have had to take a bus to China. So I stayed home with Seth while Lynn traveled on her own.

**Lynn**: We'd gotten a picture of Lindsey, but then we didn't hear from the Chinese orphanage for the longest time. I thought, "Oh no, not again!" Turns out that the Chinese government was stopping the adoption of healthy infants. They said we could get a child with medical problems instead of that little girl in the picture that we'd already fallen in love with. We were so upset. For months we had been looking at that photograph and already felt like she was our child.

**Jeff**: That was maybe the moment of our biggest disappointment out of so many. We'd made copies of that little picture and passed them around to our family and friends.

**Lynn**: And we'd refinanced the house to make the trip over there to get her. Now it seemed like she'd been taken away from us. Even though this was the fifth time we'd had our adoption plans fall though, it never got any

easier. In fact, I think we took the loss of Lindsey hardest of all. Fortunately, our adoption agency wouldn't take "no" for an answer. They went to the Chinese to protest the decision. The agency raised so much Cain that the authorities finally said, "OK, you can have your kid." When they finally placed her in my arms, she never even cried. We felt like she was meant to be our daughter. We got to go the orphanage instead of getting our children at the hotel, like usual. It's something I'll never get out of my mind. All those little toddlers running up to you. And rows and rows of cribs packed tight together, some with two babies to a crib. It seemed like there were miles of diapers on the lines. I took a picture of that. It's great to have pictures to show Lindsey where she was before she came to live with us.

**Jeff**: Now with Ilsa, we like to joke that she was our accidental adoption! Seth really wanted to have a brother but when we looked into adopting a boy from Guatemala we discovered it would cost about twenty five thousand dollars. So we knew that wasn't going to be happening.

**Lynn**: Then Gail at the adoption agency told me about a Guatemalan baby girl. Because she had a heart condition she was available immediately and the fees would be waived so she could get treatment as soon as possible. They gave me her medical records and I showed them to a doctor, who advised against the adoption. But as we had learned from Lindsey's adoption, Gail at the agency doesn't like to take no for an answer. She encouraged us to

CONSIDERING ADOPTION

get other opinion, and other doctors were more optimistic. Jeff and I finally asked Seth about it and he said, "Mama, if she needs a home, she needs to come here." Until that moment, we'd been back and forth on the decision, but that sealed the deal. We didn't have the money for travel until we got our tax rebate but when it came it was exactly the amount I needed to get to Guatemala. The attorney down there waived his fees and everyone just pitched in to make it happen.

**Jeff**: Adopting Ilsa took on a life of its own. I thought Lynn was crazy when she first brought it up, but she badgered me until I finally had to retreat to "Yes, Dear.'

**Lynn**: By the time we were able to bring her home, she was twenty months old. She was terrified. She cried and screamed for the longest time, like she was kidnapped. I told Jeff, "This is the biggest mistake we've ever made." She'd bite, hit, kick and scream for hours.

**Jeff**: She wouldn't get anywhere near me, and, like Lynn, I'm kinda thinking "big mistake.'

**Lynn**: She was sharing a room with Lindsey and having terrors all night long, so poor Lindsey wasn't getting any

sleep. It was really rough for the whole family the first couple of years we got her home. Actually, it was like hell. Every time we'd try to go somewhere, more often than not she'd fall down screaming. The poor child. The first few years she was with us she'd insist on toting all her belongings in a big bag. Even to bed. To this day she has to have the little Winnie the Pooh from the orphanage with her. At least now she's down to just a pocket book. She keeps it in her backpack when she goes to school. She goes to bed with her pocket book and bear and if she gets up in the night, they go with her.

**Jeff**: Now she's my good buddy, but she still has those awful night terrors from time to time.

**Lynn**: The therapists say she has post-traumatic stress syndrome. Even now she still sometimes has uncontrollable anger. Raising Ilsa has been a real education for us. I'd never even heard of night terrors. In the middle of the night, I'd find her standing up in the bed, holding on to the headboard, facing the wall just screaming. But like Jeff said, "Her heart can't be that bad, or it would have exploded by now!" And I'm glad to say that nowadays she's happy more often than not.

# DAN

●●●●●●●●●●●●●●●

My birth mother was a house maid in Santiago, Chile, who got pregnant by her employer. She gave me up when I was two months old. My adoptive parents went down to Chile to adopt two little girls. One of them wasn't available so I guess I was next on the list at the orphanage. I was three and a half and had been in five different foster homes before I finally landed in National Home of the Child, where I was adopted by my American parents.

They'd already adopted a boy from Korea a few years earlier, so I had a ready-made family waiting for me in West Virginia. He's only a year older than me but I idolized him. As a teen I got introduced to racism when the kids in high school made us feel like outsiders. My other brother and sister are from Chile, from the same orphanage. There weren't many Latinos or Asians in Morgantown. The disconnect is that even though I look Hispanic, I grew up on white bread and yellow mustard and don't speak a word of Spanish! I have a line that I use because I think it's funny and because it hides my shame. "I'm a spic from the sticks!" In those days, assimilation needed to be 100%. I was put in speech therapy as a kid because I rolled my S's and my R's. No traces of otherness, please.

I'm in awe of the amazing hearts of my parents. To take in four kids as your own is a true act of love. Even though I have resentments towards them, I'll always love them. Because my dad had such a financial burden supporting a wife and four kids, he wasn't around much. And when he was home he was often distracted. As I've grown older, I can more appreciate why. But as a kid I would have given anything to hear him say he loved me. Because the brunt of day-to-day child care was on my mom, we were often abused as children. When my older brother was diagnosed with cancer, the financial and emotional strain was tremendous. He survived but the family was badly shaken. We three younger kids all bear the scars we brought with us to America, so we weren't strong enough to cope with the stress. I started acting out to get attention and my other brother developed eating disorders and became suicidal. My sister was delayed developmentally and had a tough time making her way in the world growing up. By the time I was a young teenager, I was running away from home. That is, when I wasn't being kicked out of the house. And I used any kind of drug or alcohol I could get my hands on. I'm going on two years clean and sober now but I've still got the track marks on my arm.

I so wanted to be held and told I was loved by my parents but my behavior had the opposite effect. I felt like I didn't belong anywhere. Certainly not in West Virginia with all those rednecks! They're so dumb, they can't even get their racism right. They'd call me a "sand nigger," and I'm from South America!

On one hand I was raised being told that I was special, that I was chosen. On the other hand, I was paddled and told I was worthless. One time my mom made me spell "futile" between each smack. I didn't excel academically and my dad told me I'd end up being a garbage man. When I brought home yet another lousy report card, he told me to work on my grip so I wouldn't fall off the garbage truck. Education was so important in my family that we even walked to the school bus stop in the order of our grade point average. I was always last. My parents would say, "Every horse has its ass." They tried to shame me into getting good grades but all it did was shame me.

That being said, I know they wanted the best for us and were frustrated when we continually messed up our lives. As an adult, I can respect them for their good intentions but the child in me is still angry. My neediness hurts my relationships to this day. There's a hole inside me that can't be filled. I'm finally realizing that substance abuse, or even the love of a good woman, can't save me. The only thing that can repair the emptiness inside is love for myself. My fear of abandonment will never be completely gone but I need to learn to accept it as a part of who I am and work from there. There are definitely days when I don't feel loved enough. Not by my friends, my wife or, especially, myself. I have a tattoo that says, "Don't turn away." The pathetic thing is how my neediness actually drives people away. I'm finally realizing that I can't hold other people responsible for my insecurities.

I have an eight year old son from a teenage relationship. Like so many kids who are adopted, I wanted to have a child to fill the empty space that caused me so much pain. The mother was my high school love. Her parents were getting divorced after twenty years and she was as emotionally bereft as I was. We made that baby together in desperation. I was the bad guy with the good girl. She finally couldn't take any more of my out-of-control adolescent behavior and broke up with me. I was somewhere getting high when my son was born. To this day she doesn't trust me alone with him. I only have supervised visitation rights. It's a terrible thing. I've done to my son what was done to me. I've abandoned him, turned away. I have a tattoo of my son's name, but that doesn't keep me from being a deadbeat dad. I can't make enough money to feed myself, much less send child support.

Until I can get over these abandonment issues, I'm too easily derailed to be of use to anyone. I'm constantly battling my inner child. I pray that someday I can make friends with my inner eight year old and forgive both my birth and adoptive parents. As an adult, I can forgive my mother's verbal and physical abuse but the little boy in me is still angry. I still experience the loneliness that only exists in foster homes. My inner child is a confused runaway. Growing up in West Virginia, I was always looking back toward the people who abandoned me instead of forward to the family who adopted me. Bad idea.

# ANDREW AND MARY WITH BENJAMIN AND MIA

· · · · · · · · · · · · · · · ·

**Mary**:  Before we were married, Andrew and I talked about having three children. That was the picture in our heads. Ben was born four years after we were married.

**Andrew**:  Conception was the easy part for us. Pregnancy was the hard part.

**Mary**:  I got pregnant the first month we tried and the problems in my pregnancy started right away. I started spotting about a week after I took my home pregnancy test and had to have a stitch put in my cervix at twelve weeks to keep from going into early labor. I was put on partial bed rest and had to work from home. At twenty weeks I went into serious labor and was put in the hospital. They had me on three different medications trying to slow things down. When they got me stabilized, I was sent home on strict bed rest. I wasn't even supposed to work from my bed and could only get up to use the bathroom. They had me on a continuous drip of medication to delay contractions. Our magic number was twenty eight weeks. We made it to thirty weeks before it was impossible to keep from giving birth.

**Andrew**:  Ben was only three pounds, seven ounces, but he was breathing on his own. They say all those months of labor matured his lungs. Ben still had to stay in the hospital for over five weeks before we could bring him home. Even then, he only weighed four and a half pounds. The doctor told us that Mary would always have a difficult time carrying a pregnancy to term.

**Mary**:  When Ben was three and a half we knew we wanted another child. Despite the fact that the best possible scenario was that I'd be on bed rest the whole pregnancy and I'd have another preemie to care for when we had a toddler at home, we decided it was worth it. Getting pregnant the second time, however, wasn't so easy. It just didn't happen. We knew we couldn't risk the multiple pregnancy that IVF often results in. If I couldn't carry one baby to term, I was certain to lose twins or triplets.

**Andrew**:  Our decision to adopt was an evolution in our thinking that we both came to at the same time. We got to the point where we had to decide if we wanted our family to be just the three of us or if we wanted to look at other

141

options. That was a long discussion, because the three of us were really happy.

**Mary:** I wanted Ben to have siblings. I was one of six kids and felt strongly that my son should have that special bond you get from a sibling growing up alongside you. Every child needs someone they can complain to about their parents, someone who really gets it. You appreciate it even more when you're an adult. Your brother or sister can understand things about you that no one else can. Eventually we knew we'd need to adopt if Ben was going to have a sibling. He was already in third grade. The Korean program appealed to us because there was a shorter waiting period and you didn't have to travel out of the US to get your baby. We didn't want to bring Ben to Asia and we didn't want to leave him behind.

**Andrew:** Korean adoptions are built on mountains of paper work, from recommendations from our employers, friends and neighbors, to medical physicals, bank and insurance statements—even FBI background checks and fingerprints. We had home inspections and each of us had to write a ten page autobiography and take parenting classes. You're thoroughly vetted before you adopt.

**Mary:** At times it seemed a bit overwhelming, but I think the requirements were good because they made us talk about things we hadn't thought to talk about. The agency looks at your life through a microscope, from many different angles, so you do, too.

**Andrew:** When the agency finally had a baby for us we met Mia and her escort at Dulles airport. Of course, Ben was with us. When they unstrapped the baby carrier and placed her on a chair, he was the first one to move forward and touch her...

**Mary:** ...and she kicked her little legs and made raspberry noises for the sheer fun of it. Even though she's been only been in our family for two months now, she's already such a part of the picture.

**Andrew:** Her foster family in Korea made an album for us, and she looked as happy then as she is now. I assumed that she'd have quite an adjustment leaving the only family she'd ever known, but if she did, she certainly didn't let on.

**Mary:** It's as if she knew us from the first moment we were together. There were amazingly few problems adjusting to a different diet and sleep schedule. She's just a very easy baby. Ben has been wonderfully accepting from the moment she arrived. The first night she was home, he asked me if I loved Mia as much as I did him. I said I was sure that, given time, I would. He seemed satisfied with that answer. Later, when we took her for her shots, he got so upset when she cried that he's still mad at the nurses. He doesn't see her as competition. He sees her as part of his family. He's more possessive than competitive.

**Andrew:** When he plays video soccer games, he now chooses being the Korean team.

**Mary**: When the kids at school were discussing their family backgrounds, he added Korean to his heritage along with Italian, Hungarian and German, because his sister is Korean. It's been a remarkably smooth transition from three to four family members. Her grandparents are as crazy about her as we are. My mother was relieved that I didn't have to go through such a difficult pregnancy again and is thrilled to have a granddaughter.

**Andrew**: We're falling more and more in love with her every day and she's only been our daughter for eight weeks.

**Mary**: Because of the difficulty of my pregnancy, I had nine months to think of nothing but my developing baby. If I sneezed or rolled over, I had a contraction that threatened his very survival, so every waking move and thought during those months of bed rest was about Ben. I felt like I'd known him all my life by the time he was born. Even though

Mia came to us through tremendous organizational effort, it's not the same bonding experience as pregnancy, particularly a pregnancy that doesn't afford you any distraction. The first week we brought her home, I felt a little confused and guilty that I didn't have this instant love-at-first-sight connection like I did with Ben, but already she's such a part of our family, I can't imagine life without her.

**Andrew**: At first I sometimes resented her for taking time away from Ben, but as her schedule became routine and I grew ever more attached to her, those feelings quickly faded.

**Mary**: I sometimes felt the same way at first, but I'd remind myself that having another child was as much for Ben as it was for us or her. Having Mia in the family has brought out a whole new nurturing side of him. He is devotedly protective and can make her laugh more than we can.

PART ELEVEN:

RELINQUISHMENT,
ABANDONMENT AND
SELF ESTEEM

# STEVE AND JULIE WITH JOSH, JACOB AND ISAAC

● ● ● ● ● ● ● ● ● ● ● ● ● ● ●

**Julie**: When I was eighteen years old I got pregnant despite the fact I was on birth control pills. The father of my child didn't want to have anything to do with the pregnancy. At five months, he was still suggesting that I have an abortion.

I was in college and working as a writer and photographer, so I thought I was a mature grown up. In fact, I really wasn't when faced with such an awesome responsibility. I had a fatalistic attitude that if I got pregnant despite birth control the baby was meant to be.

I was afraid to tell my parents. My older brother died in a car accident when I was a teenager, my father lost his job and my mother completely shut down. My family was still reeling when I discovered I was unintentionally pregnant. I just couldn't burden them with my problems, but at the same time a part of me believed that somehow my parents would save me and it would all work out happily ever after. Around my seventh month of pregnancy, I moved back home. My mom kept mentioning that I was gaining weight and asking me if I was pregnant, but it was always in front of my brothers and sisters. I felt like she didn't really want to know. If she'd wanted the truth, she would have asked me that question when we were alone. About a month before my due date, I came home at lunchtime with the intention of telling my mother the news. She put her hands on my large hard belly and said, "Are you sure you're not pregnant?" I said, "Yes, Mother, I am pregnant!"

The first words out of her mouth were, "Well I hope you're not planning on keeping this baby. There's no way your father and I can take on raising another child at this point in our lives." When she said that, I shut down emotionally and said, "Well, I guess I'm not now!" I thought that my parents would give me the backup I needed to raise my baby. My mother obviously loved babies and I just assumed, "What's one more?" In retrospect, my parents were just trying to protect me, but I was so hurt and angry. I wouldn't wish what I went through on anyone. I'd already paid my hospital bill before I told my parents I was pregnant, because I wanted to prove to them that I was responsible enough to keep my baby.

My mother went with me for my final month doctor appointment. We told him that my plans had changed and I wasn't going to be able to keep my baby. My ob/gyn didn't try to change my mind, but instead offered to facilitate an adoption. I had no boyfriend, no parental support, no financial resources. My relinquishment was more coercion than decision. I don't consider the surrender of my baby for adoption a choice. I was a teenage girl tossed on a sea of circumstance.

When I went into labor, I was so drugged up on scopolamine that I had nightmares for twenty years afterwards. I'd dream that I was holding my baby and then someone would call my name. When I'd look down, my arms would be empty. Sometimes I'd dream I'd be screaming at a bottom of a pit, and even though I could see faces at the top, they couldn't hear me. They'd be passing my baby around, saying, "Oh, it's a girl," but they acted like I wasn't there.

They'd been trying to induce labor for weeks, but I was so shut down and reluctant to surrender my baby, that my body didn't give her up without a tremendous fight. When I woke up, I kept asking if I'd had a boy or a girl, but the nurses wouldn't tell me. It was a long day waiting for my doctor to return and give me an update.

**Steve**: When we met a few years later, she told me within the first week of our friendship that she'd given a baby up for adoption and that at some point in the future, she was going to try to contact her.

**Julie**: By the time I was twenty two, I decided I wasn't interested in guys who had no backbone. I'd lay my story out there as a test, to see whether they were worth my time.

**Steve**: I guess I must have passed the test! We were married five months after we met.

**Julie**: The ironic thing is that we were never able to conceive a child together, even though there was no physical reason. My fertility doctor suggested that I grieved so much over the loss of my daughter that my infertility was psychosomatic.

**Steve**: At the same time we were trying to have our own biological children, we were discussing adoption.

**Julie**: The idea of taking a child into your home to make a family always appealed to me, even when I was a child. I started my search for my daughter twelve years ago. It's not easy with a closed adoption—it took four years. When I finally tracked her down, our first phone call lasted three and a half hours. My birth daughter came to see me the following week, and as I was leaving to go pick her up at the airport, we got a call from social services. They had three brothers available for us to adopt. I instantly went from none to four kids. After that, my nightmares stopped. Something happened inside me and I was unblocked.

**Steve**: The minute I saw the three boys I knew they were our kids. Even though I realized we had no idea what we were getting into, I also knew it was the way it was supposed to be. They were four, seven and eight years old and in desperate need of parents. They'd already been in nine different homes. Their foster care situation was so bad that after one visit with the boys, social services asked if we were ready to commit to keeping them. We said "yes" without hesitation. They seemed excited to move in with us, yet they had a hard time trusting our devotion because they'd been passed around so much. It's taken us years to prove to them that we'll never abandon them. I can't imagine any biological parent loving their kids any more than we do ours. They're our forever kids. Well-meaning friends say they don't know how we can make such a commitment to "other people's" children, but they're not "other people's," they're ours.

**Julie**: These are our sons. We are their parents. We have the same expectations as biological parents. When you're a parent, you don't give up. You always try to do the right thing for your kids. We were told that the boys had ADHD that was treatable with medication. It was soon apparent that they had more serious problems than hyperactivity and attention deficit. They were depressed and aggressive, and had been emotionally damaged by foster parents who had told them they were ugly and stupid. They have severe learning disabilities as well as a long list of co-morbid biological disorders, including bipolar disorder, post-traumatic stress syndrome, reactive attachment disorder, and borderline personality traits.

**Steve**: People say, "Those boys are so lucky." I tell them, "I was a selfish person when I adopted these children. We did it because we wanted children.'

**Julie**: There was no altruism involved. We wanted to be a mommy and a daddy. There was no conscious thought of rescuing anybody. We just wanted to give and receive the love that can only be found between parents and children. When I hear our boys call me Momma, I get thrown back in time to the love I felt in my own childhood. Momma and Daddy are joyous words.

**Steve**: For the first six months after they first started calling her Momma, she was so overwhelmed with gratitude that she practically burst into tears. It was a strange and wonderful thing. Eight years later, it still fills me with wonder when my sons calls me Daddy.

# JEWELL COURTNEY

●●●●●●●●●●●●●●●●

My parents always told me and my sister that we were adopted. Some of their friends who had adopted didn't tell their children until they were eighteen and it caused difficulties. In fact, several of the kids absolutely hated their parents after that. They left the house and wouldn't speak to them. When you're deceived about such a fundamental truth, it's hard to trust your parents about anything else. Fortunately, my parents were more enlightened. My sister and I aren't related and the two of us look nothing alike, or like our adoptive parents. I'm much bigger than my mom and dad, and my head of blond curls started turning grey in my early twenties. My dad still has a full head of dark straight hair.

I've thought about tracking down my birth mother to see what she looks like, but was always afraid of what I might find. And it might hurt my adoptive parents feelings, so I decided I didn't care that much. My sister, however, was more troubled by being given up for adoption. As a teenager she became very rebellious. Sometimes, in fits of anger, she'd tell our mother, "I'm going to find my real mother and live with her." I felt bad for my mom.

My sister and I couldn't be more different. I'm gay and she's a religious fundamentalist. We grew up going to Methodist Sunday School but religion wasn't discussed much at home. I was always teased by the boys in school. I liked music and hanging out with my girlfriends. I've always been chubby and un-athletic. I got called "sissy" a lot. My childhood sexual experimentation and early sexual experiences were all with other boys, but they wouldn't have anything to do with me in public. I remember asking my mom what a "homo" was. She read the definition of homosexual to me out of the dictionary. I never discussed my sexuality with my parents until my sister outed me when I was in my early twenties.

My sister always resented me because I was the easy going kid who never caused any trouble. She struggled every step of the way. We never liked each other growing up because we were such total opposites. She'd become a fanatic Jesus freak by high school. She believed in the End Times and was speaking in tongues. I brought some friends down from New Jersey once to stay in my parents' house while they were out of town. We were going to attend the first gay pride march in Washington, DC. My sister was staying at our parents' house as well. She went to the march that was protesting the march I was attending. So I'm on one side of the street demanding an end to discrimination against gays while she's on the other side of the street carrying a sign saying that we are all an abomination and will burn in hell. When our parents returned home, she told them about my so-called sexual deviancy. For the first time in my life, I found myself in a screaming fight with my parents. They were shocked and horrified. My mother said it made her sick to think about what two men do with each other. I said it didn't exactly turn me on to think of my parents in bed together either, so let's not think about what's none of our business. My father told me the name my birth mother had given me and suggested I take back that name. He didn't want me to have his. It took a long time, on both sides, to get over the hurt.

My grandmother finally patched things up. She couldn't believe my parents would be so shocked by something so obvious and she confronted them about their denial. She also reminded them that I was still the same boy they'd loved all along. My parents and I are so unbelievably close now. I couldn't ask for more love and support. When I was sick with peritonitis, they slept on my futon for two weeks. I almost died from a ruptured appendix recently, and I was overwhelmed by the love and support I received

from my family and friends. The phone calls, cards and letters were simply overwhelming. My mom and dad have come to realize that gays are born that way—it's not some kinky lifestyle choice. My mom even started defending me when my sister would say I was going to hell. Now my sister and I have negotiated a truce. She doesn't talk about religion and I don't try to convince her to be more accepting of my sexuality. We agree to disagree, and we stay away from certain topics. We can finally hug each other and say, "I love you."

I've considered adopting a child but I'm not sure I'd have the ability as a single parent to invest time in nurturing while also making a living. And as a single gay man, I'd probably only be able to adopt a hard-to-place child with special needs. I don't think I'd have the patience to help a child with all that extra emotional baggage. I don't even teach music to children anymore, because I don't have the patience I used to. I also realize I'm feeling lonely since I broke up with my boyfriend and that loneliness isn't a good enough reason to become a parent. I've found myself longing for the unconditional and reliable love that I didn't get in my former relationship, but it made more sense to get a cat than a kid.

I've had self-esteem issues all my life. Being a fat sissy wasn't easy. I've had alcohol addiction problems and suffered with depression for a large part of my life. I've always been trying unsuccessfully to fill a void. I often find myself in emotionally abusive relationships with

other men. I've always felt this emptiness, a black hole that can never be filled. I think that sense of emptiness and loss result from the fact that you're in this woman's body for nine months and as soon as you emerge from the womb, you're whisked away and are never able to gaze into her face or be held in her arms. Then you're cared for by nurses and foster parents until you're adopted, which I finally was at eight months. My adoptive mother told me that my foster mother didn't want to give me up and the social workers had to come take me away. I imagine I was also equally attached to her and must have felt a great loss then. I suspect that's been at the core of the abandonment issues I've always struggled with. In my romantic relationships, my neediness often drives people away. I now realize I was self-medicating with alcohol. I'm on medication for depression and insomnia and I no longer drink. I feel loved by my family and friends, as well as my pet cat. Life is good.

Music is one of the greatest joys in my life. I started piano lessons at five and could play by ear from the beginning. I've been a church organist since I was a teenager. Today I'm the choral director as well as the organist. The first time I heard the organ at National Cathedral I knew that was the instrument for me. I just fell in love with the sound. I might have inherited my musical ability from my biological parents, but it was my adoptive parents who always encouraged my talent.

# JACOB HECTOR

•••••••••••••••••

I was born in Medellin, Colombia. My parents named me Hector Guillermo Diaz Henao. The first eight years of life was very hard for me and my four sisters. We were so poor, we often didn't have any place to live. And when we did, my mom would lock us in the house while she went off to the streets. That was in the days of Pablo Escobar, when drugs and crime infected every part of the city. Everyone was either using or selling, or both. Our family was constantly on the run from the police. My older sister and I took care of the three littler ones and did what we could to keep everyone alive and together. We'd sit outside of restaurants and watch people eat until they'd feel bad enough to give us the leftovers. We were always sick with worms and disease.

My dad got arrested with my two youngest sisters when they were only two and an infant. The girls were put in a foster home when dad went to jail. When I visited him there, he taught me how to snap my fingers and whistle. That's all I can remember him ever teaching me. We knew the police were looking for mom, so my two other sisters and I never stayed any place long. I remember when a white station wagon came up. We were caught, and the four of us were put in this little cage in the back. She fought like crazy, because mom could be really mean and violent, but she couldn't escape. We cried until we realized that life was going to be so much better for us in a foster home. We had a bed and food and I was reunited with all four of my sisters. We always had a strong bond because growing up with my parents on the streets all we had was each other. Our parents didn't leave us with any happy memories. It was nice to be taken away from them. They were scary.

The five of us loved living with our foster parents, who were kind. We got Christmas presents for the first time. Of course we didn't know about adoption or the United States. All we knew was what was right in front of us. Soccer was my one joy. After about a year with our elderly foster parents in Medellin, a letter came from a family in America who said they wanted to adopt all five of us. They sent pictures of their nice house and themselves with their other kids. We were excited. We'd never seen anything like the house they lived in. Our new adoptive father came to Colombia and flew all of us back to the United States. Our

> **Adopting me and my four sisters was an overload for our adoptive parents. We were angry and afraid after our life in Colombia. With eleven adopted children in one family, it's impossible for one mom and dad to give those damaged kids all the attention and guidance they need after years of deprivation. —Jacob Hector**

adoptive parents didn't speak any Spanish and encouraged us not to speak it among ourselves, so we could learn English quicker. School was hard at first, but we had tutors who helped us learn the language. Today our English is much better than our Spanish. My younger sisters can hardly speak Spanish at all.

Our adoptive family had four biological kids and eleven of us that were adopted. We were the last five to arrive. I think adopting me and my four sisters was an overload for our adoptive parents. We were angry and afraid after our life in Colombia. With eleven adopted children in one family, it's impossible for one mom and dad to give those damaged kids all the attention and guidance they needed after years of deprivation. The first year was such a shock, so different from anything I'd ever known, that I can't remember much about it. Even though I was picked on at school for being different, I got along okay at home with all my new brothers and sisters.

Unfortunately, I never got along very well with our American parents. We were always arguing about something. To this day they still believe I stole money from them when I was thirteen. There's nothing I can say to make them trust me. I had a lot of anger that I'm sure wasn't their fault, but it often spilled over into my

relationship with them and at school. Kids there would call me "spic" and "wetback," and I'd get into fights. My English tutor befriended me and would invite me to spend time on her farm. By the time I was fourteen, I worked for a friend's dad, selling snow cones on the beach. My adoptive parents owned apartments and we kids would work there after school and on weekends. I moved out of their house when I was sixteen, working thirty five hours a week to support myself on top of a high school course load. They turned my younger sister over to social services. I'll never forgive them. There were things that happened within my adoptive family, things I can't talk about, that were unforgivable. I knew I had to move out before I hurt someone.

I don't want to make it sound like adoption is a bad idea, because it's not. It can be a great thing to do. I just think in this case our parents had too many kids with too many problems. I'm thankful that I came here and I respect my parents for adopting the five of us, but I don't think they lived up to the responsibility. One part of me feels grateful to my adoptive parents for taking us off the streets. Another part feels betrayed. You know what they say about good intentions? The road to hell is paved with them!

# AMY

•••••••••••••••••••

I was born in Seoul, South Korea. My father died a few months after I was born. My birth mother didn't have much education and it was hard for her to make a living and take care of me at the same time. By the time I was a young child, I'd been shuffled among different relatives' homes. I remember feeling lonely and missing my mother. Every time she had to go back to work, I'd chase her down the road crying. When I was eight, she got a job as a gardener out in the country, where we could live together in the gardener's cottage. She was determined to get me a good education and somehow she sent me to school in the city two hours away. The four hour daily commute was just too exhausting, so she arranged for me to stay with the teachers on school days and spend the weekends with her. I had a stomach ache every time I was supposed to go back to school.

One day my mom asked me if I'd like to go to America. She said I could go if I was adopted by an American family. I had no idea what that meant, but I was like most young Koreans and really interested in the United States. The more she told me about being able to live with both a mother and a father, and maybe brothers and sisters, the more appealing it sounded. Even though I didn't like being separated from my mother, I'd gotten pretty used to it. I didn't realize that she wouldn't be able to come visit me because it was so far away and so expensive to get there. I just thought about the fact that I wouldn't have to move around all the time and be so lonely. We met with the Love the Children Agency. When I saw a picture of my adoptive family in America, I remember getting really excited, especially about having a little brother.

My mother took me to the airport and I boarded a plane with lots of infants who were also going to America to get adopted. I was thirteen years old at the time. I didn't even cry, because I had no idea what was happening. Once I realized how far away I was traveling, it began to dawn on me that I wouldn't be seeing my mother for a long time. I was crying by the time we landed in Japan, but had calmed down by the time we got to Chicago. On the flight to New York, I put on the traditional Korean costume that my birth mom had packed for me so I'd be wearing it when I met my adoptive father at the airport. We couldn't talk to each other because I only spoke Korean. We arrived at their house in the

Washington, DC, area. I met my new mother and my new baby brother smiled at me right away. I loved that! I so needed to have a stable family that I loved them right away. At first it felt awkward to have a father. As much as I'd always wanted one, I wasn't sure how to behave once I did! Over time I got more comfortable. When Halloween rolled around the first year, I already had my costume—the traditional dress that my mother had sent me over here in.

Luckily in Northern Virginia there is a lot of diversity in the schools and a lot of kids who spoke Korean. The transition wasn't too difficult, except at first all the Americans looked alike to me! In the English as Second Language classes, I didn't feel out of place because everyone was in the same boat, even though the others weren't in the process of getting adopted. I made friends in the neighborhood as soon as I could speak English. I didn't like it when my adoptive mom got a job in Texas and we had to move. There were no Asians there at all and I felt out of place. I was so glad when we moved back to Northern Virginia. The crazy thing is after a year or so in this country, I started thinking in English and forgot my Korean.

When I was in my late teens, my Korean mom somehow saved up enough money for me to go back to Korea. After seven years away, I'd almost forgotten all my Korean, but after a week it started coming back. My mom eventually moved to California. After my daughter was born, I took her there to meet my birth mom.

I was twenty five and engaged to Elizabeth's father when I got pregnant. Having her made me really get focused. I realized that if I married her father there'd always be tension between us and I didn't want to raise my daughter in that environment. He may not have been right for me, but he's still her father and I encourage them to have a close relationship. Elizabeth is close to his mother as well. She's twelve years old now and has great relationships with all of her grandparents. My birth mother married in California and my adoptive parents have divorced and both have remarried. My American mom had two more kids and we all go on vacations together.

People often ask me if I'm mad at my birth mom for handing me over to another family at 13. I can honestly say that I was old enough to understand that she did it for me, not for her. It was terribly hard for her to do. She never had to tell me so, I saw it in her eyes. She wanted to give me a better life. I've been able to send Elizabeth to the same school system from kindergarten through sixth grade. By having a more financially secure life in America than my mother was ever able to have in Korea, I've been able to give my own daughter the childhood I always wanted.

PART TWELVE:

ROOTS AND
THE SEARCH
FOR IDENTITY

# JOEY WITH DAN AND KATHLEEN

●●●●●●●●●●●●●●●●

*(Joey speaks first, before being joined by his parents.)*

**Joey**: I have happy memories of my early childhood in Minnesota. We lived near my dad's side of the family and my parents would have parties with the relatives. My older sister was in high school then and she and her friends would babysit me. I was like the little baby doll they could dress up and parade around. I was four when we moved here to Montana and I hated it. I missed my extended family. I remember the trauma of starting kindergarten. They had to pry me off my mom's leg. To this day, I'm not crazy about school. It was there I realized I was the only kid with different color skin. It wasn't until years later that it occurred to me to ask my parents why I looked different from them or the kids at school. When I did ask, they painted a rosy picture of me being a blessing from God and them picking me out at the hospital.

I'd be interested to know who my birth parents are. What Indian tribe they're from and what they're doing now. But it's not a driving obsession. If I was able to meet my birth mother, what I'd really like to know are the circumstances of my birth. Why couldn't she keep me? If I'd stayed and had a terrible family life, I'd probably be angry as hell at my biological mom. Even so, I'd like to hear her side of the story before passing judgment.

It's lonely being one of only five people of color in my entire school, especially when I'm the only one who looks like me when I get home. My parents can't understand how I feel like I'm on the outside looking in. They run a hotel and know everyone in town. Of course, everyone knows who I am, but people don't really know me. I've put myself out there so many times to make friends only to get rejected. Over the years it makes you isolated and withdrawn. I was never picked to be on teams on the playground or invited to anyone's birthday party. By middle school, I realized that the only time kids were nice to me was when their parents and teachers made them—which of course, only made the kids hate me more. It's no better in high school. At least at seventeen, I can get in my car at noon and go to lunch alone instead of sitting by myself in the cafeteria. I've never been on a date and probably never will as long as I'm in my high school.

No girl would want to go to the prom with me. It would do nothing to enhance her popularity.

Even though I know my parents can't do anything to change the behavior of the kids at school, I still wish that they'd never brought me here in the first place. This isn't a good place for someone who's different. I'm hoping when I go to college I can go out of state, to a place where I could blend in—not stick out like a sore thumb. I have a loving relationship with my parents, but I need to move into a bigger world. Even though it's tough being so isolated in a small-minded town, my mom and dad are pretty decent parents. For so many years, I used to hope we'd move back to Minnesota. I've grown to accept the fact that they are going to stay and I'm not.

I don't mean to sound sorry for myself. I'm just trying to be honest. I know without struggle you can't succeed and that adversity can make you stronger. Maybe I'm just one of those people whose best years are not high school. I probably look forward to the future more than the popular kids do, because I can't wait to get out of here.

*(Joey's parent, Dan and Kathleen, join him and the conversation continues.)*

**Dan**: We got married when Kathleen's daughter, Jessica, was seven years old and I adopted her. During that process we got to know the social workers. Kathleen is part American Indian and Social Services told us about a part-American Indian baby that needed a home. Five days later he was our son.

**Kathleen**: Joey's foster parents had wanted to adopt him but regulations in Minnesota didn't allow foster parents to adopt infants in their care. If they could, very few babies would become available for adoption outside of the foster care network. I don't think the fact that I'm a small part Native American had much to with our being able to adopt him. Actually, we didn't give his ethic background much thought. He was our baby boy and we loved him. I remember once when he was playing with Danny, his blond-haired, blued-eyed cousin, in a doctor's waiting room. Another child pointed at Joey and asked, "What is he?" Danny had no idea what the question meant. He shrugged and said, "He's just Joey." My brother-in-law—Dan's brother—had adopted an African American, a Korean and an Eastern Indian child, so Joey's appearance was never an issue in his family.

**Dan**: We know that Joe's had a tough time fitting in at school as he's gotten older. People don't see Joe, they see a large, dark skinned male. Our African American niece had the same problem in high school. She was never once asked on a date.

**Kathleen**: Joe's never even tried to blend in. Maybe because he knows he can't. He was the first kid in school with dreadlocks. Seventeen year olds are often not very

comfortable in their own skins, but they can usually shore up their insecurities by surrounding themselves with friends. Joey hasn't got the security of people his age who he trusts.

**Dan**: One place where Joe fits in well is as an uncle. His sister and her son live nearby and they have the sweetest relationship. He's got pictures of his nephew in his bedroom and an extra bed for when he wants to stay over. He's not afraid to show love for his family, which is something a lot of teenage boys aren't very good at. He never complains to us about the isolation he feels in school but of course we notice how much time he spends alone. But when kids do call, he often doesn't call them back.

**Kathleen**: He's always been an old soul—the proverbial still waters that run deep. He's rarely silly, but often passionately opinionated. We're proud of Joe's uniqueness and I think, in a way, he is too. Joey's solitude is less alarming to us because his big sister Jessica was the same way. She tended to stick to herself. For her, though, it was a choice, and for him, it's imposed. It's hard on his self-esteem to be so isolated, but I believe in the long run he'll be fine—more than fine. When we took him to New York City, he loved it, and wasn't in the least intimidated by the hustle and bustle. He'd hail the cabs and give the cabdrivers the directions. He just fell right into place in the city, full steam ahead. When I asked him what he liked most about it, he said it was that everybody looked different. Not that everyone looked like him, but that everyone looked different. He absolutely loved it.

# BOB

•••••••••••••••••••

I was adopted at birth. Growing up I remember being read a book called *The Adopted Child*. I never had a negative thought about being adopted, probably because I was placed in my adoptive parent's arms hours after I was born. They were always open about my adoption, so there were no secrets or shame. That was not always the case for the birth mother back in the early fifties. My parents had all the information about my birth mother, so when I had questions about her, I could contact her. Oddly enough, I never gave my biological parents much thought at all until after I was married and had children of my own. My wife encouraged me to search things out and I'll be forever grateful for her intuition and insight.

I started out being a responsible parent in search of my genetic history for my children's sake. However, once I began the process it became as much an emotional as a medical issue for me. It's overwhelming, really. Your thoughts are consumed by a thousand questions and possibilities. A reunion with your birth mother begins to answer questions you didn't even know you had. I had no idea what to expect, except that she was willing to meet with me. When the agency asked Dot for permission for me to contact her, they reported that the first words out of her mouth were, "Oh, my baby boy!" Introspection is not my strong suit, but when I heard her reaction I realized that this was going to get heavy. The reunion would be about much more than idle curiosity and a medical history.

After a letter and a brief phone conversation, my wife Holly, and my children joined me on the drive to Dot's home in Asheville, North Carolina. But they stayed behind while I drove to the address she'd given me. When I got there, there was an older woman sitting on the front porch. When I saw her face, I instantly knew she was my mother; the physical resemblance was startling. I think I expected to feel some molecular pull, some instant and magical connection, but truthfully, there wasn't any. There was only a woman in her seventies who looked like me. I gave her a hug and waited for this lightning bolt of maternal electricity, but nothing happened except an awkward embrace. There was a sense of sadness between us for the lost forty years, but it was fleeting.

When I walked in her house, there were only two pictures on her wall: a picture of Jesus and the picture of me with my family that I sent her after I first spoke with her.

Later I introduced her to Holly and our children and she introduced us to her big, extended family. They immediately embraced us as part of their big family. One afternoon she walked me down to the local drugstore, where all the little old ladies with their oversized pocketbooks hung out for coffee. She was beaming as she introduced me to her friends. Most of her friends hadn't known about me until I showed up on the scene, but I was treated like a king. Everyone seemed impressed by my very existence. I'll never forget the sense of pride it gave me.

Dot was reticent about telling me the story of my conception, but I eventually pieced things together. She was in the process of getting a divorce and living in a boarding house where she met a younger man, who was a medical student. Her quote about the liaison was very discrete, "Well, it was just one of those things, honey." Now, whenever I hear that expression, I think, "So am I! I'm just one of those things!"

I appreciate the impossible situation she was in—divorced and pregnant in a small southern town in the nineteen fifties. She left town to work for a doctor in Farmville, Virginia. This doctor knew my parents and put them in touch with Dot. So she knew during her pregnancy with

me that there were adoptive parents waiting to raise me. Still, it must have been a terribly hard time for her. It was like *The Scarlet Letter* all over again. The social sanctions against single motherhood were so strong back them, it would cast shame on an entire family. My birth mom never remarried or had any more children. Just me.

Getting to know her sister and her family, I learned where I got my quirky sense of humor. I also learned that getting to know me as an adult was a rejuvenation for Dot. I was told that she'd become increasingly withdrawn and depressed as she grew older. Getting to know her was rejuvenating for me as well. It began to answer some fundamental questions about who I am. Being adopted is like having an old cedar chest in the attic. One day you have to get up in there where it's dark and musty and start digging around, looking for clues. I also had to confront the fact that my mother never held me and that my father remains a complete enigma.

I grew up near the ocean with two loving parents who were always open and honest with me, but I still have important issues about rejection and self-esteem. I was never really aware them of until I began the relationships with my own biological family. It's been an interesting voyage of self-discovery; I still have a lot to learn. When Dot was dying in an Asheville hospice, I came down to see her. When I arrived, the hospice worker said, "Are you Bob? She's waiting for you. She's been hanging on until you got here." She was non-communicative, but I

sat on her bed and just started talking. I don't know what I said, except that I loved her. As soon as I got back to my hotel nearby, the phone rang. She had died peacefully. Her "baby boy" felt the loss, but was grateful to get to know her before her death.

While I think I know who my biological father is and where he lives, I haven't made contact with him yet. I'm not sure he knows that I exist. He was told of my mother's pregnancy, but he denied being the father and wouldn't have anything to do with her. One of these days I'm going to knock on his door, look in his eyes and say, "You don't have to come out and play catch with me, but I want you to see me. I do exist!" The potential is there for him to slam the door, but it's a risk I feel that I should

take. I won't disrupt his domestic life. It's interesting that I haven't done it by now and I'm more than a little anxious. Adopted people who never search for their biological parents may fail to do so because they're afraid of what they might find.

Even though my parents were always grateful for my adoption, they were more than a little uncomfortable when I actually met Dot and formed a bond with her. It was important to me that the three of them meet, and they did, even though I know it was hard for everyone involved. I felt how simply happy Dot was that day. They even posed for a picture with their arms around each other. My only real regret is that I did not get to know Dot sooner.

# HEIDI

●●●●●●●●●●●●●●●

My adoptive parents lost a baby and didn't conceive again for ten years. They decided to adopt when they learned about my twin sister and me, who were being raised by my birth mother's mother. We were a fifteen months old when we were adopted. Our birth mother was a teenager who didn't want us to be raised by her mother because she felt like she couldn't get on with her life if we were always around. From what I understand, our maternal grandmother wanted to keep us but our mother insisted that we be adopted. A month after we were adopted, our adoptive mother got pregnant after ten years of trying. So our sister was born while we were still babies. It was all too much for our adoptive father, and he left three months after our mother gave birth to our younger sister. I don't remember him ever being around.

My twin sister and I grew up feeling like we were mistakes, not only for our birth mother but our adoptive mother as well. She'd never have adopted us if she knew she was going to give birth to her own daughter. Growing up, my twin sister and I felt like unwanted houseguests. We were afraid of our mom. By the time we were teenagers, I started getting angry at how unfairly we were treated. I was more outspoken than my twin and would defend myself more. Even though we were twins, we look nothing alike. She's shorter, darker and stockier than me. Both of us were treated so differently from our younger sister that it was glaringly apparent. Our mom would introduce her three girls by saying, "These are my adopted twins and this is my daughter."

A week before high school began, my mother sent me to my aunt's house to live. It hurt to be sent away but it was a relief to have someone to talk to. It felt nice to be treated like a good person. I always felt like a bad kid around my mom. But then my mom fixed up a special bedroom for me and said things would be different if I'd come back home. Like a fool, I believed her. To this day, the room has remained empty. She never let me or anyone else move into it. The room was set up as a privilege that I was never good enough to deserve.

Things went from bad to worse. My mom's obsession with cleanliness became like the movie *Mommy Dearest*. My twin sister and I kept competing for our younger sister's favor, in hope that our mom would be more loving towards us as well. She'd have birthday parties for our younger sister, but not for us. When she'd get mad at me, which was almost always, she'd lock me outside in the cold without warm clothes. I'd go to school with bruises and be obviously emotionally distraught. But when people asked me what was wrong, I never told anyone. I was still desperate for my mother's love, because it was so unattainable. I was afraid that if I was taken out of her home, nobody else would want me either. I sought out my birth mother at this time, but that was a big disappointment. Even though we looked a lot alike, she wasn't someone I could admire. She was on welfare and a real "poor me" pity person. I didn't need to mother another mother, so there was nothing for me there.

At fifteen, I got the courage to leave home. I wrote my mom a letter saying I was leaving so home life could be better for my sisters. I moved in with a friend's family and for the first time in my life I was happy. Going to their house after school was something I looked forward to instead of dreading. After six months there they called a social worker to come get me and put me in a foster home. The Massachusetts Social Service's objective is to reunite families whenever possible, so it wasn't long before I was having visitation with my adoptive mother. We continued to argue, even on short visits. After one visit, I was so depressed that I stayed in my room at my foster home for days, not even eating or drinking anything. Finally

I walked out the front door while my foster mother yelled at me, "If you leave this house, you'll be considered a runaway." I was just going to a friend's house, but I was picked up by the police and given the choice of going back to my adoptive mother's house or being placed in a runaway shelter.

Still wanting the unattainable, I moved back in with my adoptive mother. Nothing had changed between us. My mother had the social worker give me a psychiatric evaluation, and when I was told that I wasn't crazy and that my biggest problem was my mother, I felt stronger than I had in ages. I was no longer so desperate for my mother's approval.

I moved out of her house and in with the family where my twin sister was staying. I stayed there for a year and a half. I felt safe and secure there and made plans for college. I was accepted at three out of the four places where I applied. I got a financial aid package and for the first time started feeling acceptable and focused, finally getting enough self-esteem that I felt hopeful about the future. During that time my sister got us on *The Montel Williams Show*, during a program about kids who had never met their biological fathers. We actually met our birth dad on the show. He said he never believed he was our father but agreed to a paternity test, which proved that he was, in fact, our biological father. He looked a lot like my twin sister, except he was tall like me. It meant a lot to both of us to see the physical characteristics that we'd inherited from him, but he couldn't really be a father to us.

Getting through college was a long bumpy road, but I got my degree in speech and marketing while working my way through school. I met my husband there. I probably shouldn't have married him, but I didn't have the inner strength to say no. I had five people from my side at the wedding and he had about a hundred and thirty. My sisters were there but my adoptive mother wouldn't come. Even though he was almost a complete stranger, my biological father did walk me down the aisle. I didn't feel happy on my wedding day, but love had never been easy for me to come by, so there was no way I would refuse my husband's proposal. That's not a good reason to get married. My husband's a great guy, but I shouldn't have married him.

I need to feel safe on my own, and not dependent on his love. I feel really bad about hurting him, but guilt is not a reason to stay married either. I'm at a place in my life now where I feel enough love for myself that I no longer feel I have to get it from someone else to feel worthy.

I also know I don't love my husband as much as he deserves to be loved, and that I need to set him free. It's both a selfish and selfless act to let him go.

I feel like for the first time, Heidi's all here. I'm not making decisions based on fear and insecurity.

I don't know if I'll ever get over trying to prove myself to my adoptive mother. I still want her approval. Maybe that's OK, because it drives me to be successful. I hope one day I'll be able to heal the pain from my childhood by having children and giving them the childhood I always longed for. I'd love to have a daughter that looks like me and give her all the love I never had. Every child is so vulnerable to their parents and so needy for their love. I have no doubt that adopted children can thrive if they're raised in a loving and nurturing environment. But I also think that many adopted kids have a real struggle coming to terms with their identity, even in the most caring of homes. When I started that struggle in adolescence, my adoptive mother just didn't have the ability to deal with it.

# CYNTHIA AND WAYNE WITH DEANNA

• • • • • • • • • • • • • • • •

**Wayne**: We were in our early thirties when we got married after a long friendship and a short courtship. We both deeply value our families, so it was an unspoken assumption that we'd have a family. After about six months of not conceiving, we went to the doctor and discovered that I was shooting blanks.

**Cynthia**: There are risky and expensive procedures like in vitro fertilization that we could have tried, but we quickly got comfortable with the idea that we weren't going to have biological children. I think it was a harder decision for Wayne than for me.

**Wayne**: Yes, I did have a harder time letting go of the idea of fathering my own biological children. It took me longer than it did Cindy to give up that idea. She moved on through that grief period and accepted our inability to conceive a baby much more quickly than I did. When you grow up in this country as a white middle class male, you feel like you're in control, whether you are or not. My sterility shook that perspective. One thing that helped me through it was discussing my feelings with Cindy. Sterility felt like a threat to my identity—of what it means to be a man. It might be irrational, but it took me six months to even begin to feel good about myself and look forward to the adoption process. I couldn't switch my expectations with the snap of a finger but by the time I was ready to adopt, I was truly ready.

**Cynthia**: I know that Wayne felt guilty then for not being able to get me pregnant. This was something he put on himself because I didn't feel that way at all. I know a lot of women want the experience of pregnancy and childbirth. Because of my professional medical background, I had seen it up close and didn't have any romanticized notions about the process. In fact, I was kind of relieved! I happily embraced adoption as our destiny. When a co-worker at my hospital adopted a daughter from China, she shared her experience of the whole process with me which made it easier when it was my turn.

**Wayne**: We didn't want to adopt domestically because of the risk that the birth mother would change her mind and not relinquish the baby. We knew that would break our hearts. Once we decided to go the Chinese adoption route, we did things a little differently. We went on our own instead of in a group. We wanted to extend the trip so it would be less grueling.

**Cynthia**: My friend who had been there us told us about the long trip and getting the babies as soon as they arrived. It was exhausting. I worried that I'd look so bedraggled that our baby would take one look at me and run!

**Wayne**: If we were going there and bringing back a Chinese child, we wanted to be able to tell her about what we had seen in China. We couldn't do that if we had no time to adjust to the jet lag or couldn't spend time looking around before we got our baby. Because, of course, once we had our baby, we'd be too absorbed to see anything else. We took pictures at the Great Wall and other landmarks that we still share with her.

**Cynthia**: By the time we got to China, we'd received five different pictures of DeAnna, from three to thirteen months, so we knew what she looked like. When the people from the adoption agency arrived at the hotel lobby with the children, we immediately recognized her. All the other parents recognized their kids too. It was a joyful occasion. They put her in my arms, and there she stayed for the next six months. She didn't want me to put her down. We just clung tightly to each other.

**Wayne**: We were like the animals in the forest. Cindy could carry DeAnna around without even enfolding her

in her arms—she just stayed tightly wrapped to her side. From that moment on, we felt like parents.

**Cynthia**: She was like one of those dolls that cries when you put them down, so I just held her. Back in the States, I'd do housework with DeAnna on my hip. I held her so long and so often that I developed inflamed tendons in my wrists.

**Wayne**: I'd stayed home full time the first eight weeks after we brought her home. I worked at night after DeAnna went to bed and Cynthia worked out of the house three or four days a week. It took us a while to figure out the best way to parent while making a living.

**Cynthia**: We thought it would be ideal to have both of us work part time. In hindsight, we would have been better off if one of us stayed home and the other worked full time. It was so stressful and exhausting for both Wayne and me…

**Wayne**: …though it was probably perfect for DeAnna. She always had at least one of her parents, but it was hard on the two of us because had no private time together. When we tried to put her in daycare, it was obvious that she still needed to be with us. She hadn't gotten her bonding needs met when she was a baby, so she was making up for lost time. For the first few years, Cynthia and I were like two ships passing in the night.

**Cynthia**: She did wonderfully at any social activity as

long as we were there. It was hard on us both until she got to preschool. She's thriving there now—really loves it. She's as possessive of her best friend, Rosie, as she is of us. We live in a town with another little girl from the same orphanage in China and DeAnna immediately bonded to her. They're like sisters.

**Wayne**: We moved from Sanford to Chapel Hill, NC, because ten percent of the school population here is Asian. We wanted to send DeAnna to school with other kids who look like her. Even though I don't see her as Asian—I just see her as my daughter—other people do. Until we moved to Chapel Hill, people were always staring or asking us questions. The population in this university town is so much more diverse. That she's Asian and we aren't isn't a big deal here.

**Cynthia**: The school system here has Chinese language immersion programs and Saturday Chinese culture classes. We both think it's important that we raise her to embrace her Chinese heritage. She knows that she's Chinese by birth and that we're not.

**Wayne**: She'll be four in June, and she loves to watch her adoption video over and over! We want her heritage to be something that she's aware of from the beginning. That

PART THIRTEEN:

WHEN THE
BIOLOGICAL FAMILY
REUNITES

# ANNE AND KARINA

**Anne**: When I was twenty one, I moved to Europe to live with my sister and work. Shortly thereafter, I realized I was pregnant. I had begun living with a man who I eventually married, but he wasn't the father. For me, raising the baby wasn't an option even though my then-boyfriend would have supported a decision to keep the child. I had no desire to be a mother then. In fact, I never did. Giving her up for adoption was the obvious solution. I was introduced to an American military couple in Germany who wanted to adopt and I lived with them for the last month of the pregnancy. They were the sweetest people. One of the best decisions I ever made was letting them be Karina's parents. The proof is sitting right here in front of you. They were wonderful parents and she had a great upbringing.

**Karina**: I knew the story of my adoption from as far back as I can remember—that Anne had lived with my parents before I was born. Back then, women didn't have friends or family in with them when they gave birth. My mom used to joke that she was mopping the floors when I was born. Because my parents were so open and comfortable about adoption, I never felt weird about it. In fact, I've always felt like a princess, the chosen one.

**Anne**: After the adoption I built my own life, as did Karina's family. But ten years ago I got a phone call from her adoptive mom. Karina had some medical problems and needed to know her family medical history.

**Karina**: I was twenty six years old, and it took us less than three days to track Anne down. I was the adored only child of great parents and never had any interest in meeting my birth mom—until, that is, we needed information about my biological family's medical history. Mom asked Anne if I could contact her. When she agreed, I discovered that I couldn't wait to speak with her. Our first conversation, on the telephone, lasted for hours. My parents offered to fly me to see her for my birthday a few months later.

**Anne**: Except for my sister who had been in Europe with me twenty six years ago, no one knew that I had a child. When Karina and I decided to meet, I told the rest of my family about her existence. I knew my friends would be supportive. If they weren't, I wouldn't want them as friends anyway!

**Karina**: Even though neither one of us is touchy/feely sentimental, we embraced quite easily for a long time when she picked me up at the airport. After meeting Anne, I realized I'd been missing something, but I didn't realize what until we met. I always believed more in nurture than nature until I met Anne and her sisters. They felt like family as soon as we met. Getting to know them didn't undermine my relationship with my parents at all. It just made me feel more complete.

**Anne**: It was an amazing experience to go to the airport and see myself, but twenty years younger. I hadn't spent my life mourning her loss, but it sure felt good to put my arms around her. It gave me a sense of completion that I hadn't realized I needed. Having Karina in my life now hasn't made me regret giving her up. We got together when the time was right for both of us. When she came for a later visit with her husband, he was amazed by our similarities.

**Karina**: It's not just how we look. It's also our mannerisms—the way we move our hands and the inflection of our voices.

**Anne**: Our reunion was successful because Karina was raised by loving and generous parents. Getting to know her reinforces that I made the right decision those decades ago. Even though I am her biological mother, Karina's mom is back in Ohio.

**Karina**: I think of Anne as a close friend who gave birth to me! I love coming out here to be with her. Getting to know her and the rest of her family helps me know myself. I get to have more aunts and uncles and cousins than anyone deserves. Now that I've recently lost both my dad and my grandmother, I feel even more grateful to have both my mom and Anne.

# TIM

●●●●●●●●●●●●●●●●

My work as a writer keeps me constantly on the road. I spend a lot of time with back packs, sleeping on the ground, climbing mountains, running rivers, crawling around in caves—basically enjoying myself by putting myself in some degree of jeopardy. Ever since I was a boy in Wisconsin, I wanted to be a writer. I was always involved in sports in school, but also had this dream of supporting myself through writing. After I got my MFA in creative writing back in the sixties, I published some pieces in the San Francisco Sunday Magazine that got the attention of Rolling Stone. I got a job there as an editorial drudge and within a few months was writing my own articles about rock and roll stars. Since I was one of two people in the office at Rolling Stone who liked to go outdoors, I was involved with the creation of Outside Magazine at the onset.

As I was traveling all over the world, I always assumed that one day I'd be a husband and a father. I was involved with a woman for a long time who had fertility problems, and that strain was probably part of the reason we broke apart. I didn't get together with my wife now until she was in her forties, so neither one of us had much expectation of being parents. By the time I was in my early fifties, I realized I'd probably never be a father.

Back in the sixties I got my girlfriend pregnant and we'd given the baby over for adoption. We were terrified and overwhelmed. It was a big secret from everyone but our parents. She went to a home for unwed mothers. We told our friends and family that she was on a trip to Spain. When she got back home after the birth, we continued to date as though nothing had happened. I have to admit, in hindsight, I probably wasn't as sensitive as I should have been to what she'd been through. I just felt grateful to get our life back on track and assumed she was too. Like typical mid-westerners of that time, the pregnancy and adoption was something we never talked about. Over the years we'd say something like, "Oh my God, our son is six years old today," and then we'd both fall silent for quite a while.

After college she moved to San Francisco with me when I was working out there. She began to have symptoms of schizophrenia, but I had no idea why she was hearing voices and becoming paranoid. Back then there was no medication for the disease and they tried to treat schizophrenia with talk therapy. The therapist of course wanted to talk about the adoption, but we now know that giving a baby up for adoption doesn't cause a chemical imbalance in the brain. Her condition continued its downward spiral because all the talking in the world wasn't going to help. She was eventually institutionalized. I'd come by to see her every couple of years. She could remember everything up until the time the disease took hold of her in her early twenties better than I could, but nothing much after that point.

I can only imagine my son, Todd's, concern when he sought out his birth mom and discovered a mentally ill woman, enormously obese from the medication for her illness. By then her mind was pretty muddy but she could remember me clearly because of the years we spent together before her illness. Todd at first tried to contact me through my publisher but that letter languished in oblivion. He eventually got a contact letter to me through a co-writer friend of mine. As soon as I saw his birth mother's name and his date and place of birth, I knew my son had found me.

I felt it was my duty to write him back immediately. I was going to be near where he lived in Denver for the IMAX opening of the film, *Everest*, which I co-wrote, so I invited him to come. I was doing a reading while I was there and he came to that. I recognized him immediately. He looked just like me at his age, except he had his mom's blond hair and blue eyes. When we met, he laughingly said, "What a screw job! I got your receding hair line, but not the height!" When I went to visit him at his house, I immediately noticed that he drove the same model car and even grilled on the same brand grill that I do. He loves to cook, just like I do. Like me, he's works out almost every day. It was a unique experience to be in the company of a complete stranger who seemed so familiar. He showed me pictures of his childhood. He obviously had a much better life than his birth mother and I could have offered. When we discussed what his childhood might have been like if we had raised him, both of us realized that it was the best thing for everyone that he was adopted. Even so, there's residual guilt. Flesh and blood is a powerful obligation.

When I told my parents about Todd tracking me down, they had more regrets than I did and said, in hindsight, they wish they had been courageous enough to raise him themselves. By the time my son contacted me, they were in their eighties and were no longer intimidated by the

morals of thirty five years ago. Todd brought his wife and two daughters to Arizona to meet my parents on several occasions. When my dad was terminally ill, he made a heroic effort to sit and visit with them three days before he died.

My wife has been incredibly excited and delighted about the whole experience of Todd's appearance. She loves it when the girls call her Grammie. Life has a different path for everyone. Out of the blue in my fifties, I have not only a son and wonderful daughter-in-law, but I get the privilege of watching my two granddaughters grow up. I lost my parents in the same five years that I gained a son and grandchildren. The Lord has given and the Lord has taken away.

# ELIZABETH WITH ELIJAH, ISAIAH AND JOSHUA

**Elizabeth**: When Elijah was born twenty two years ago, I was an unwed teenager with no alternative but to place him for adoption. Eighteen years later, after I had married and had two more sons, Elijah came back into my life.

**Elijah**: I never remember a particular moment when my parents told me I was adopted. It was something I always knew from the beginning. When I was sixteen, I got a birthday card from my birth mom and I realized that she lived nearby.

**Elizabeth**: I'd been sending him cards every birthday and holiday but he never got them. I chose Elijah's adoptive parents with the understanding that they'd keep me updated on his growing up, but the first time I heard from them was when he was six or seven years old. They sent me a Christmas card with a photo of him and his adoptive sister. My name was spelled wrong on the envelope. That really crushed me. It made me feel like a nobody. But I can't began to describe how much that picture meant to me. When Elijah entered his teens, he was getting in trouble at school and having a hard time at home. His parents contacted me and asked me to write him a letter that might help him with his struggles. All kids struggle with their identity growing up and I think it's sometimes even more complicated for adopted kids. When I relinquished him to his family, I gave them a box filled with keepsakes from my pregnancy and a letter written about the love from which he was conceived. And I explained why it wasn't in his best interest to be raised by a single mom.

**Elijah**: My parents gave me the box when I was going through a hard time. I'd been expelled from school and decided to drop out. They weren't very happy with me and I wasn't very happy with myself. I always felt different from my family when I was growing up and I always resented the rules in school. I had a hard time fitting in. The contents of that box helped me feel a connection, though, to something that had been missing in me. As soon as I turned eighteen, I decided to seek out my birth mom.

**Elizabeth**: When I was pregnant with Elijah, my parents were going through a divorce and my fiancé had walked out on me. Giving him up was my cross to bear for eighteen years before he contacted me and said he wanted to meet. From that moment on I began for the first time to feel like an integrated woman, that a part of me wasn't missing. I could say, "I'm the mother of three sons.'

**Elijah**: The only way I can describe how it felt when we met again after eighteen years is "perfect." It felt perfect. I couldn't believe our similarities—her love of music and nature and working hard outdoors.

**Elizabeth**: I knew that things would never be the same again. That very day he told me I had a grandchild on the way and he took me to meet his girlfriend, and her mother and grandmother and sister and cousins. All of a sudden, my world just expanded. I told him he had two brothers, but Isaiah and Josh were still so young, I didn't rush in to telling them about their big brother until I figured out the best way to approach it. When my mother suddenly had to have surgery, I realized it might be my last chance for her to see her firstborn grandson and new granddaughter. Of course, I couldn't leave my other two sons at home, so the circumstances meant that everyone would meet.

**Isaiah**: Even though it was weird at first to discover I had a brother who I never knew existed, it also felt completely natural to hang out together.

**Joshua**: I was so excited to meet him once I found out he existed. It was great to suddenly have an older brother!

**Elijah**: I wanted my daughter to meet her biological grandma too. Kids can never have too much love. The more family, the better, I say. My adoptive parents and I have gotten along really well since I moved out of the house. I know I put them through a hard time. Now that I'm a parent myself, I'm grateful for all they did for me.

**Elizabeth**: I was devastated all those years when his adoptive parents didn't keep in touch with me, but I now realize they did what they thought was best for Elijah. We have that bond of all wanting to do the right thing for him. Several years ago, his mom came by on Mother's Day with a collage of Elijah's childhood photos. It was a gift for all the years I patiently waited in silence, until they were ready to share him with me. She thanked me for giving her the opportunity to be a mother. I treasure that Mother's Day gift and the rapport I now feel with Elijah's mom. It's my wish that one day adoptions will be more open, and that birth parents and adoptive parents can support each other and work together to see that the child's needs are met.

I've met so many people through the years who've been adopted. They love to hear my story of how I made the decision to give my baby to adoptive parents. I focused my thoughts on what was best for my baby. My mother wanted me to keep Elijah and move in with her, but I would have been caught in the middle of my parents' divorce. I wanted to keep my baby with every cell of my being but I made myself think of others first. I knew that was the right thing to do. If I'd been older, I might have been strong enough to fight convention and raise him on

my own. At seventeen, I didn't have the resources to stand up for my own maternal instincts, which, of course, were as strong for Elijah as they were for Isaiah and Josh.

People who are adopted need to know that their birth mothers aren't cold hearted and selfish. Many of us gave our babies to adoptive families out of love and unselfishness. We want what any mother wants—what's best for our baby. Because my own family was falling apart and my boyfriend left me, it was especially important to me that Elijah have a secure family structure, with a mother and a father who could nurture him financially and emotionally.

The hardest day of my life was when his adoptive parents came to take him to their home. I was trying to be positive, so I thought that Valentine's Day, the day of love, would be the perfect day to give this gift to this lovely childless couple. His mother brought me a jar of homemade jelly which symbolized that she would be a mother to my son. I knew they were ecstatic, but I was completely stunned. It felt like being hurled into a grief that had no end. For days I could barely speak. It took years to find my voice and speak about my experiences. My constant prayer was always that Elijah would be OK and that one day he'd want to meet me. Something was broken inside of me until he renewed his relationship with me at eighteen, the same age as when I gave birth to him. For eighteen years, I never felt deserving of being loved. I'm sure that's part of the reason my marriage to Isaiah and Josh's father failed. Once Elijah was back in my life, I focused all my energy on my three sons and stopped dating for years. I needed time to heal—to forgive myself and feel worthy again. Now I enjoy the love of a wonderful man and can love in return since I feel whole.

I can't express the joy I felt attending the births of Elijah's children. When the doctor handed me the scissors to cut the cord, I passed them over to my first born, now a man. My heart was filled with gratitude knowing that I'd have the privilege of watching his children grow up.

ABOUT
THE
AUTHOR

# About the Author

Mary Motley Kalergis is an author, photographer and interviewer, whose work bears witness to the bonds that connect individuals, families, and communities.

Her published books include *Love In Black & White* (Dafina Books, Kensington Publishing), *Charlottesville Portrait* (Howell Press), *Seen and Heard: Teenagers Talk About Their Lives* (Stewart Tabori, & Chang), *With This Ring: A Portrait of Marriage* (The Chrysler Museum of Art), *Home of the Brave* (E.P. Dutton), *Mother: A Collective Portrait* (E.P. Dutton), and *Giving Birth* (Harper & Row.)

Her photographs have been featured in numerous anthologies and collections including Aperture's *Mothers and Daughters*, Pantheon's *Generations*, Stemmle's *In Their Mother's Eyes*, National Geographic's *Star Spangled Banner*, Fawcett's *In Celebration Of Babies*, and Andrews McMeel's *Waiting for Baby, Reflections* and *The Enduring Circle of Love.*

Her work has been exhibited in museums and galleries internationally, including The Smithsonian Institution in Washington, DC; The Burden Gallery and the International Center of Photography in NYC; The Chrysler Museum of Art in Norfolk, Virginia; The Virginia Museum of Fine Arts in Richmond, Virginia; the Southeast Museum of Photography in Daytona Beach, Florida; The San Antonio Museum of Art;, The Field Museum of Chicago; the *Museum Fur Photographie* in Stuttgart, Germany and the *Diaframa Kodak Galleria* in Milan, Italy.

Photographs by Mary have also appeared in newspapers and magazines around the world, including *The New York Times, People, Time, Newsweek, Glamour, Ladies' Home Journal, Seventeen Magazine, Sports Illustrated, Marie Claire* (France), *The Guardian* (London), and *Camera Manuchi* (Japan).

Mary was formerly on the faculty of The International Center of Photography in New York and has served as "special stills" photographer on movie sets.

She lives in Charlottesville, Virginia, where she is currently finishing her ninth book, *Foxhunters Speak*, to be published by Atelerix Press in 2016.

CPSIA information can be obtained at www.ICGtesting.com
Printed in the USA
BVIW12n2306130515
399696BV00001B/1